What got you here won't get you There

Praise for *Power of a Positive No*

"William Ury brings a marvelous blend of experience, insight, integrity and warmth to his work. In this wonderful book he teaches us how to say No—with grace and effect—so that we might create an even better Yes."
—**Jim Collins, author of *Good to Great***

"Every woman needs a copy of this book. Learning to set realistic limits while honoring relationships is more than a win-win strategy. It's a miracle. I promise that learning to deliver a positive no can change your life—it changed mine dramatically in a single week."   —**Joan Borysenko, Ph.D., author of *Inner Peace for Busy People* and *Inner Peace for Busy Women***

"For me and many others who are involved in resolving disputes, a new book by Bill Ury about negotiation is an exciting event. This incisive new approach will be a boon to all of us."   —**President Jimmy Carter**

"William Ury's advice on how to say 'No' gracefully brims with social intelligence. An immensely useful book for anyone."
—**Daniel Goleman, author of *Social Intelligence***

"Born of profound professional worldwide experiences and painful personal challenges, this is another marvelous book from William Ury, really a prequel to *Getting to Yes*. It compellingly shows that you can give a 'positive no' if you find the burning 'yes' inside you.... Tremendous contribution!"
—**Stephen R. Covey, author of *The 7 Habits of Highly Effective People* and *The 8th Habit: From Effectiveness to Greatness***

"The world's biggest shared secret is that most of us say yes when we really want to say no.... Bill Ury generously provides us with insights and techniques to turn this malady into win-win solutions. This is a wise and powerful book."   —**John Naisbitt, author of *Megatrends***

"No matter whether you are negotiating compensation with the toughest CFO or a curfew for your teenager, this book teaches us a critical and counterintuitive lesson. You *can* say no and still be *nice*. Simple, straightforward, and easy to read, *The Power of a Positive No* is a YES on our reading list."   —**Linda Kaplan Thaler and Robin Koval, authors of *The Power of Nice: How to Conquer the Business World with Kindness***

"If I'd had and used this book for the last twenty-five years, I would have doubtless avoided innumerable heartaches and headaches and tattered personal and professional relationships.... This all-important book stands alone on a subject that underpins, like no other, individual and organizational effectiveness."   —**Tom Peters, author of *In Search of Excellence***

"Yet another essential roadmap from Bill Ury . . . this book is the perfect companion to *Getting to Yes* and should be read by anyone who struggles with getting what you want while continuing to protect that which is most important to you. Be prepared—this book will change your life."
—**Anthony Robbins, author of *Awaken the Giant Within* and *Unlimited Power***

THE
POWER
OF A

How to Say No

POSITIVE NO

and *Still* Get to Yes

WILLIAM URY

Bantam Books

THE POWER OF A POSITIVE NO
A Bantam Book / March 2007

Published by
Bantam Dell
A Division of Random House, Inc.
New York, New York

Grateful acknowledgment is made to the following for permission to reprint work:

Ilan Shamir, Advice From a Tree, © 1993–2004 YTN. Reprinted by permission.
www.YourTrueNature.com Your True Nature, produces inspiring tree books, journals,
posters, and The Gift of a Tree greeting cards. All are printed on recycled paper and 100%
replanted. Workshops and keynotes also offered. Contact: www.YourTrueNature.com or toll
free 1-800-992-4769.

Henry Jacobs, © 1975, 4 Dobson CD recordings "Terry Dobson Teaches," from
www.wattstapes.com

Richard St. Barbe Baker, "The Man of the Trees," is quoted with the permission of
Richard St. Barbe Baker's Literary Executor, Hugh Locke, of Hugh Locke Associates, Inc.

Path To War, HBO film, is reprinted by permission from Home Box Office, Inc.
Screenwriter Daniel Giat.

Book design by Susan Hood

Bantam Books is a registered trademark of Random House, Inc., and the colophon is a
trademark of Random House, Inc.

Library of Congress Cataloging-in-Publication Data
Ury, William.
    The power of a positive no : how to say no and still get to yes / William Ury.
       p.   cm.
    ISBN-13: 978-0-553-80498-0
    1. Negotiation.   I. Title.

    BF637.N4U795 2007
    158.2—dc22   2006043015

Printed in the United States of America
Published simultaneously in Canada

www.bantamdell.com

BVG 10 9 8 7 6 5 4 3 2

FOR LIZANNE,
LOVE OF MY LIFE,
WITH ETERNAL GRATITUDE

Contents

Acknowledgments

"You took *five* years to write this book?" my eight-year-old daughter Gabriela recently asked me in a tone of disbelief.

"Yes," I replied.

"More than *half* my life?" she asked.

"Yes."

"What is there to say? All you have to do is say No. It's simple," she said. "And you don't have a grabby lead," she added.

"What's a grabby lead?"

"The first sentence is supposed to grab the reader's attention. Yours doesn't," she said.

"Oh." It was humbling.

Those who point out our shortcomings are our most benevolent teachers—and Gabriela is certainly one of mine. I feel deeply grateful to each of my many benevolent teachers for all the many lessons that have served me so well as this book was written.

Let me begin with my colleagues at Harvard's Program on Negotiation, a place that has served as my intellectual home for the past twenty-five years. In particular, I feel very fortunate to have had as my mentors Roger Fisher, Frank Sander, and Howard Raiffa, and as my early colleagues and friends David Lax, Jim Sebenius, and Bruce Patton. I would also like to thank our chairman Robert Mnookin and managing director Susan Hackley for sustaining and strengthening the Program. And I owe a special debt to my colleagues Doug Stone, Daniel Shapiro, and Melissa Manwaring who made invaluable and incisive comments on the manuscript.

No one has worked harder with me on this book than Joshua Weiss, who has been my colleague at Harvard for over a decade. From the book's inception, Josh helped with detailed research, and then, as the book took form, with patient readings and useful feedback on at least seven separate drafts. A talented teacher, Josh also helped design the executive seminar at Harvard, which we developed together with the book. My pleasure in working with Josh is exceeded only by my debt to him.

I am also much indebted to Donna Zerner, who early on served as an engaging interlocutor, inspired editor, and encouraging author's friend. At a later stage, Louise Temple and Rosemary Carstens also gave me the benefit of their instructive comments and editing.

I find stories a powerful way of conveying points. I am grateful to Elizabeth Doty, a master at eliciting people's stories, who gathered numerous examples of saying No from her own interviews and experience, and also offered valuable practical feedback. I would also like to thank Candace Carpenter, Alexandra Moller, and Cate Malek for their careful research and Katia Borg for her artful help with visuals.

My early readers played an essential role in making this book easier for future readers. Mark Walton gently but firmly insisted on simplicity, constantly invoking the magic number three. My sister Elizabeth Ury, with keen ear and discerning eye, brought me back to the original title and the original governing metaphor of the tree. I am also indebted to the helpful feedback I received from my friends John Steiner, Joe Haubenhofer, José Salibi Neto, Ira Alterman, Mark Sommer, and Patrick Finerty. The book also benefited from stimulating walks in the mountains with my friends Mark Gerzon, David Friedman, Robert Gass, Tom Daly, Mitch Saunders, Bernie Mayer, and Marshall Rosenberg—and in the Brazilian forest with my brother-in-law Ronald Mueller.

For the last two years, Essrea Cherin has served as my executive assistant with high skill and unfailing good spirits, protecting my writing time zealously. I would also like to express my deep gratitude to Kathleen McCarthy and Christine Quistgard, my assistants for many years before. And, for a writing refuge in snow and sun, I would like to thank the good-hearted people of Aspen Winds.

No book succeeds without a good editor. I have been extremely fortunate to work with Beth Rashbaum, whose sensitive editorial touch and gentle urgings to include more of my personal experiences have much improved this book. Let me also record my debt to Barb Burg for her infectious enthusiasm and keen ear for the right framing; and to Irwyn Applebaum and Nita Taublib for believing in the potential of this book.

I also benefited from a savvy and accessible agent, Rafe Sagalyn, who, together with his colleagues Eben Gilfenbaum and Bridget Wagner, diligently and skillfully sought the right home for this book here in the United States and throughout the world. I am grateful to each of them.

On a personal note, I want to acknowledge my profound gratitude to a longtime mentor and family friend, John Kenneth Galbraith, who passed away within the last weeks, for his generous spirit and inspiring example as author and teacher. Nor can I fail to mention a deep debt to my friend and teacher Prem Baba for his precious wisdom in matters of heart and spirit. I am grateful to him beyond measure for many hours of inspiration and insight.

Let me end as I began with my family. I feel extremely lucky to be the father of Christian, Thomas, and Gabriela, who, together with their loyal canine companions Flecky and Miki, have grown up with this book and whose life experiences have informed it. In raising them, my wife Lizanne has succeeded in balancing Yes (love) and No (firmness) with consummate skill. The secret I have learned from her is that true firmness (No) is not the opposite of love (Yes) but actually comes from love and goes toward love. She has been my greatest teacher in the fine art of saying No. I owe more than I can say to her love and devotion, and I dedicate this book to her with all my heart.

I owe one last acknowledgment to my elders: my parents Janice and Melvin, who gave me life and love, my parents-in-law Anneliese (Oma) and Curt (Opa), who have welcomed me with open arms into their family, and my beloved great-aunt Goldyne who, now approaching 102, has long known the secret of saying No—positively!

William Ury
Boulder, Colorado
June 2006

THE POWER OF A POSITIVE NO

Author's Preface

GETTING TO NO

 If your baby gets even a cold, she could die," the doctor announced almost offhandedly to my wife and me as we were finishing an appointment. My wife was cradling our infant daughter Gabriela in her arms. Our hearts froze with fear. Gabriela had been born with serious problems in her spinal column, and this doctor's appointment was only the beginning of what would prove to be a long journey through the medical system—hundreds of consultations, dozens of treatments, and seven major surgeries in seven years. While our journey is still ongoing, I am happy to write that, despite her physical challenges, Gabriela is healthy and happy. Looking back over the past eight years of negotiating the maze of doctors, nurses, hospitals, and insurance companies, I realize how the process has called on all of the skills I have learned over the years in helping others get to Yes with their negotiation issues. I also realized that, for me personally, the key skill I needed to develop to protect my daughter and our family was saying No.

It began with saying No to the communication style of doctors who, however well intentioned, created unnecessary levels of fear and anxiety in the hearts of parents and patient. It continued with saying No to behaviors such as medical residents and students barging noisily into Gabriela's hospital room in the wee hours of the morning and treating her as if she were an inanimate object. In my work life, it meant saying No to dozens of invitations, requests, and urgent demands to give my time, precious time I needed to spend with family or researching medical issues.

But my Nos needed to be nice. The doctors and nurses, after all, had my child's life in their hands. They themselves were under huge levels of stress in a dysfunctional medical system that limited them to spending only a few minutes with each patient. My wife and I needed to learn to pause before responding in order to make sure that our Nos were not only powerful but respectful.

Like all good Nos, ours were in the service of a higher Yes, in this case a Yes to our daughter's health and well-being. Our Nos, in short, were intended to be not negative but *positive* Nos. They served to protect our daughter and create the possibility of a better life for her—and ourselves. We were not always successful, of course, but we learned over time to be more effective.

This book is about the crucial art of delivering a Positive No in every area of life.

I am, by training, an anthropologist—a student of human nature and behavior. I am, by profession, a negotiation specialist—a teacher, consultant, and mediator. I am, by passion, a seeker of peace.

Ever since I was a child, witnessing quarrels at the family dinner table, I have wondered if there was a better way of dealing with our differences than destructive arguments and fights. Going to school in Europe, only fifteen years after the end of the Second World War, with the memories still alive and the material scars still visible, made me wonder all the more.

I grew up in the generation that lived under the threat, seemingly distant but constantly present, of a third world war, one that put humanity's very survival in question. We had a nuclear bomb shelter at school, and late-night conversations with friends about what we wanted to do with our lives sometimes ended up in speculation about whether we would even have a future. I felt then and feel even more strongly now that there has to be a better way of protecting our societies and ourselves than threatening one another with mass destruction.

In pursuit of answers to this dilemma, I became a professional student of human conflict. Not content to remain only an observer, I sought to apply what I was learning by becoming a negotiator and mediator. Over the past three decades, I have worked as a third party trying to resolve situations ranging from family disputes to coal mine strikes, corporate conflicts, and ethnic wars in the Middle East, Europe, Asia, and Africa. I have also had the opportunity to listen and give counsel to thousands of individuals, and hundreds of organizations and government agencies, on how to negotiate agreement even under the most challenging circumstances.

In the course of my work, I have witnessed the huge waste and needless suffering destructive fights can cause—broken families and friendships, ruinous strikes and lawsuits, and failed organizations. I have been in war zones and seen the terror that violence strikes in the hearts of innocents. Ironically, perhaps, I have also seen some situations that made me wish there was *more* conflict and resistance—situations where spouses and children were silently suffering abuse, employees were being grossly mistreated by their bosses, or whole societies were living in fear under the yoke of totalitarian dictatorships.

From my base at Harvard's Program on Negotiation, I have worked on developing better ways to deal with our differences. Twenty-five years ago, Roger Fisher and I co-authored a book called *Getting to Yes,* which focuses on how to reach an agreement that is beneficial for both sides. It became a best-seller, I believe, because it reminds people of the commonsense principles they may already know but often forget to apply.

A decade later, I wrote *Getting Past No* in response to the most common question I received from readers of the first book: how do you negotiate cooperatively when the other side is not interested? How do you get to Yes with difficult people and in difficult situations?

Yet over the years, I have come to realize that getting to Yes is only half the picture—and it is, if anything, the easier half. As one company president, a client of mine, told me, "My people know how to get to Yes—that's not the problem. It's saying No that's tough for them." Or as long-term British prime minister Tony Blair put it, "The art of leadership is not saying Yes, it's saying No." Indeed, not long after *Getting to Yes* was published, a cartoon appeared in the *Boston Globe*. A man in a suit and tie was asking a librarian for a good book on negotiation. "This one is quite popular," the librarian answered, handing him a copy of *Getting to Yes*. "Yes isn't what I had in mind," the man countered.

Up to this point, I had been working on the assumption that the chief problem behind destructive conflict was an inability to get to Yes. People didn't know how to reach agreements. But I was missing something essential. For even when agreements are reached, they are often unstable or unsatisfying because the real underlying issues have been avoided or smoothed over, the problem only deferred.

I slowly came to appreciate that the main stumbling block is often not an inability to get to Yes but a prior inability to get to No. All too often, we cannot bring ourselves to say No when we want to and know we should. Or we do say No but say it in a way that blocks agreement and destroys relationships. We submit to inappropriate demands, injustice, even abuse—or we engage in destructive fighting in which everyone loses.

When Roger Fisher and I wrote *Getting to Yes*, we were responding to the challenge of adversarial conflict and the increasing need for cooperative negotiation in families, at work, and in the larger world. The need for getting to Yes clearly remains. But now, the more immediate and pressing need is for people to be able to say No in a positive way that enables them to stand up for what they value without destroying their relationships. No is of equal importance to Yes and indeed is the precondition to saying Yes effectively. You cannot truly say Yes to one request if you cannot say No to others. No, in this sense, comes before Yes.

This book, *The Power of a Positive No*, completes what I have come to think of as a trilogy that began with *Getting to Yes* and continued with *Getting Past No*. Where the focus of *Getting to Yes* is on *both* sides reaching an agreement, and the focus of *Getting Past No* is on the *other* side, overcoming their objections and resistance to cooperation, the focus of *The Power of a Positive No* is on *your* side, on learning how to assert and defend your interests. Since the logical sequence is to start from your own side, I have come to see *The Power of a Positive No* not so much as a sequel to the other two books but more like a prequel. *The Power of a Positive No* provides a much-needed foundation for *Getting to Yes* and *Getting Past No*. Each book stands alone, yet complements and enhances the others.

I see *The Power of a Positive No* not only as a negotiation book but as a life skills book, for all of life is a dance of Yes and No. Each of us every waking hour is called upon to say No, whether to friends or family members, to our bosses, employees, or co-workers, or to ourselves. Whether and how we say No determines the very quality of our lives. It is perhaps the most important word for us to learn to say gracefully and effectively.

A word about language: I will use the term "the other" to refer to the other person or other side to whom the No must be said, and the demands of grammar notwithstanding, I will use it with the antecedent "they" to avoid having to say "he or she," or to choose one gender over the other. I will also capitalize the words "No" and "Yes" in order to highlight their importance and relationship.

And a word about culture: While saying No is a universal process, it can take different forms depending on the local culture. Certain societies in East Asia, for instance, put a premium on avoiding the use of the word No, particularly in the context of close relationships. People do say No in these societies, of course, but in an indirect fashion. As an anthropologist by training, I have deep respect for cultural differences. At the same time, I believe that the basic principles of the Positive No apply across different cultures, understanding that the particular techniques for implementing the principles will vary somewhat from culture to culture.

Let me conclude with a note about my own learning journey. Like most people, I find it challenging to say No in certain situations. In both my personal and professional lives, I have said Yes when in retrospect I found myself fervently wishing I had said No. Sometimes I have fallen into the trap of attacking or avoiding when I would have been much better off engaging the other side in healthy conflict. *The Power of a Positive No* reflects what I have learned from my own life as well as what I've seen and experienced during thirty years of working with leaders and managers all around the globe. My deepest hope is that you, the reader, will learn as much from reading this book about the essential art of saying No as I have from writing it.

Introduction

THE GREAT GIFT OF NO

"A 'No' uttered from deepest conviction is better and greater than a 'Yes' merely uttered to please, or what is worse, to avoid trouble."

—*Mahatma Gandhi*

N*o*. The most powerful and needed word in the language today is also potentially the most destructive and, for many people, the hardest to say. Yet when we know how to use it correctly, this one word has the power to profoundly transform our lives for the better.

A Universal Problem

Every day we find ourselves in situations in which we need to say No to people on whom we depend. Imagine all the occasions for No that might plausibly arise in the course of an average day:

Over breakfast, your young daughter begs you to buy her a new toy. "No," you respond, trying to hold the line, "you have enough toys." "Please, pretty please, all my friends have one." How can you say No without feeling like a bad parent?

When you arrive at work, your boss invites you into her office and asks you to work through the weekend to complete an important project. It is the very weekend you and your spouse have been looking forward to for some much-needed getaway time. But it is the boss who is making the request, and your promotion review is coming up very soon. How can you say No without undermining your relationship with your boss and jeopardizing your promotion?

A key customer calls up and asks that you deliver the product three weeks ahead of schedule. You know from past experience just how much stress this will create internally and that, in the end, the customer may not be happy with the quality of the product. But it is your key customer and they will not take No for an answer. How can you say No without spoiling the relationship with the customer?

You are at an internal meeting and your boss's boss turns angrily to your co-worker, attacks her work scathingly, insults her personally, and humiliates her in the most abusive fashion imaginable. Everyone is silent, fearful, frozen, but secretly glad that it's someone else who is the target of abuse this time. You know the behavior is utterly inappropriate, but how can you possibly speak up and say No?

You come home to find the phone ringing. It is a neighbor and friend, asking if you will serve on a charity committee. The cause is a good one. "You have exactly the skills we need," your friend cajoles. You know that you are already overcommitted, but how can you say No without feeling bad?

Over dinner that night, your spouse raises the problem of your elderly mother, who has reached an advanced age where it is not safe for her to live alone and who wants to come live with you. Your spouse is adamantly opposed and urges you to call your mother and tell her No. But how can you say No to your own mother?

You watch the evening news. It is filled with stories of violence and injustice. Genocide is taking place in a far-off country. Children are dying of hunger while food is rotting away in warehouses. Dangerous dictators are developing weapons of mass destruction. How are we as a society going to say No to these threats? you wonder.

Just before you go to bed, you put the dog out and he begins to bark loudly, waking up the neighbors. You order him to stop, but he won't listen. Even with the dog, apparently, it's not easy to say No.

Sound at all familiar?

All these situations have one thing in common: in order to stand up for what counts, satisfy your needs or those of others, you have to say No to a demand or request that is unwelcome, a behavior that is inappropriate or abusive, or a situation or system that is not working or not fair.

Why No, Why Now

Saying No has always been important, but perhaps never as essential a skill as it is today.

In the course of my work, I have had the privilege to travel the world extensively, visiting hundreds of workplaces and families in dozens of societies and speaking with many thousands of people. Wherever I go, I see people under increasing levels of stress and pressure. I meet managers and professionals who are being burned out by overwork. I see people struggling to juggle work and family, with a particularly heavy burden on women who work outside the home. I encounter parents who find little quality time to spend with their children, and I find children overloaded with homework and lessons, with less and less time for carefree play. Everywhere people are overloaded and overwhelmed. I count myself among them.

Thanks to the knowledge revolution, we have more information and more choices than ever before. But we also have more decisions to make and less time to make them as the pace of life picks up greater speed with each so-called labor-saving technological advance. The boundaries between home and the workplace are eroding as work reaches people by cell phone and e-mail, anywhere anytime. The rules are also eroding and the temptation to cut corners and bend ethical standards is powerful. Everywhere people are finding it hard to set and maintain boundaries.

No is today's biggest challenge.

The Three-A Trap

No may be the most important word in our vocabulary, but it is the most difficult to say well.

When I ask the participants in my executive seminars at Harvard and elsewhere why they find it challenging to say No, the most common answers I receive are:

"I don't want to lose the deal."
"I don't want to spoil the relationship."
"I'm afraid of what they might do to me in retaliation."
"I'll lose my job."
"I feel guilty—I don't want to hurt them."

At the heart of the difficulty in saying No is the tension between *exercising your power* and *tending to your relationship*. Exercising your power, while central to the act of saying No, may strain your relationship, whereas tending to your relationship may weaken your power.

There are three common approaches to this power-versus-relationship dilemma:

Accommodate: We Say Yes When We Want to Say No

The first approach is to stress the relationship even if it means sacrificing our key interests. This is the approach of accommodation. We say Yes when we want to say No.

Accommodation usually means an unhealthy Yes that buys a false temporary peace. I give in to my young daughter's demand for a new toy to avoid feeling guilty that I am denying her something she wants, only to find that it just leads to more and more demands—and both of us being trapped in an endless unhappy loop. When the boss asks you to work over the very weekend that you and your spouse have been planning to get away, you grind your teeth and give in, fearing you will lose that promotion you want, even if your family life suffers. All too often, we go along to get along, even if we know it is not the right decision for us. Our Yes is actually a destructive Yes, for it undermines our deeper interests.

Accommodation can also hurt our organizations. Take an example from Chris, a participant in one of my seminars: "I was working on a huge $150 million deal with colleagues at my company. We had worked very hard on it and thought we had done a good job. Just before the deal was finalized I decided to double-check the numbers one last time. As I did the calculations, it became all too clear that the deal was not going to be profitable for us over the longer term. Because everyone was so excited about it, and people could not wait to make it official, I couldn't bring myself to throw a wrench into the works. So I went along, knowing that the project was bad for us and that I should speak up. Well, the deal happened and, as I had feared, a year later we were cleaning up a huge mess. If I had that situation in front of me now, I have no doubt I would speak up. It was a costly but valuable lesson."

Think about Chris' fear of throwing "a wrench into the

works" particularly because "everyone was so excited about it." We all want to be liked and accepted. No one wants to look like the bad guy. That is what Chris was afraid would happen if he brought up the uncomfortable facts. Everyone's excitement would turn into anger against him, or so he feared. So he proceeded to OK a deal that he and others later came to greatly regret.

There is a saying that half our problems today come from saying Yes when we should be saying No. The price of saying Yes when we should be saying No has never been higher.

Attack: We Say No Poorly

The opposite of accommodation is to *attack*. We use our power without concern for the relationship. If accommodation is driven by fear, attack is driven by anger. We may feel angry at the other for their hurtful behavior, or offended by an unreasonable demand, or simply frustrated by the situation. Naturally we lash out and attack—we say No in a way that is hurtful to the other and destructive of our relationship. To quote one of my favorite lines by Ambrose Bierce: "Speak when you are angry, and you will make the best speech you will ever regret."

Consider what happened in one large business dealing between a state government and a large corporation the state had hired to build and run a computer system to manage the state's payments to the poor, elderly, and sick. A quarter of the way through the year, the computer system had eaten up half of the state's available budget. Naturally fearful that the budget would soon be exhausted, the state officials canceled the contract and took over the project from the company. The officials were angry at the company, and the company managers in turn were angry at the state, each blaming the other for the problem.

The state officials were nevertheless interested in acquiring the computer and its database from the company because of all its valuable information. The estimated value of the computer system was $50 million. To the company, which had no alternative use for the system, the value of the system was nothing if they could not sell it to the state. To the state, the system was easily worth the $50 million because trying to re-create the data might cost them more—and besides, they did not have the time. Normally, an agreement would not have been at all hard to reach since it was in the interest of both sides. However, because each side's anger led them to attack with destructive Nos, the negotiations descended into finger-pointing. Each side stood up for itself by attacking the other. The result was no agreement and $50 million in value going up in smoke. Ten years later, the state and the company remained locked in litigation, spending hundreds of thousands of dollars a year on legal expenses. Both sides ended up losing heavily.

If many of our problems come from saying Yes when we should be saying No, surely just as many come from saying No but saying it poorly as the state government and its corporate supplier did. We live in a world in which conflict is ubiquitous—at home, at work, and in the larger society. Think of family feuds, bitter strikes, boardroom fights, or bloody wars. Each time people attack each other, what message are they really delivering? At the heart of every destructive conflict in the world, small or large, is a No. What is terrorism, the great threat of today, if not a terrible way of saying No?

Avoid: We Say Nothing at All

A third common approach is avoidance. We don't say Yes and we don't say No; we say nothing at all. Avoidance is an exceedingly common response to conflicts today, particularly within families or organizations. Because we are afraid of offending others and drawing their anger and disapproval, we say nothing, hoping that the problem will go away even though we know it will not. We sit at the dinner table with our partner in cold silence. We pretend that nothing is bothering us at work when in fact we are seething with anger at our co-worker's behavior. We ignore the injustice and abuse inflicted on others around us.

Avoidance can be costly not only to our personal health, producing high blood pressure and ulcers, but also to our organization's health, as problems fester until they become unavoidable crises.

Avoidance, in whatever domain of life, is deadening. As Martin Luther King Jr. once said, "Our lives begin to end the day we become silent about things that matter."

The Combination

The three A's—accommodation, attack, and avoidance—are not just three separate approaches. Usually, one spills over into the other, resulting in what I call the three-A trap.

We all too often start by accommodating the other. Then, naturally, we begin to feel resentful. After suppressing our feelings for a while, there comes a point when we suddenly explode, only to feel guilty afterward at the destructive impact of our attack. So we lapse back into accommodation or avoidance, ignoring the problem and hoping it will disappear. We are like a mouse caught in a maze, rushing from one box to another but never getting to the cheese.

All three approaches were at work in the crisis that hit Royal Dutch Shell in April 2004, when it was revealed to have over-reported its oil reserves by a whopping 20 percent. The company's public reputation was damaged, and its credit rating was reduced, while the chairman, the head of exploration, and the chief financial officer all lost their jobs.

The reason for the false reporting was the chairman's insistence that a barrel in oil reserves be recorded for every barrel pumped out of the ground—to which no one had the courage to say No, despite the clear evidence that what he was demanding was insupportable. Shell's head of exploration tried to raise the alarm but, pressured by the chairman, publicly accommodated even if he privately bristled. The tensions boiled over a year later when, after the chairman gave him a negative personnel evaluation, he counterattacked with a blistering e-mail message that surfaced publicly: "I am becoming sick and tired of lying about the extent of our reserves issues and the downward revisions that need to be done because of far too aggressive/optimistic bookings."

While the chairman attacked and the head of exploration alternated between accommodation and attack, the chief financial officer resorted to avoidance, hoping that somehow the problem would go away. But it didn't and, in the end, resulted in a huge mess with severe consequences for all involved.

The Way Out: A Positive No

Fortunately, there is a way out of the trap. It requires you to challenge the common assumption that *either* you can use power to get what you want (at the cost of relationship) *or* you can use relationship (at the cost of power). It calls on you to use *both* at the same time, engaging the other in a constructive and respectful confrontation.

This was what a man I will call John did when he felt compelled to stand up to a domineering father, who also happened to be his employer. John worked in the family business, putting in long hours that kept him away from his wife and children, even at holiday times. Although John's workload and responsibilities far exceeded those of his co-workers—his three brothers-in-law—his father paid everyone the same salary. It was all about avoiding favoritism, his father explained. Fearful of confronting his father, John had never complained, although he privately fumed about the overwork and inequity. Finally, John realized something had to change. Summoning all his courage, he decided to speak up for himself.

"We were at a family dinner when I told Dad I wanted to speak to him privately. I told him I wanted to be with my family during the upcoming holidays, that I was not working overtime anymore, and that I wanted to be compensated proportionately for my work."

John spoke strongly, yet respectfully. The father's response was not what the son feared it might be: "Dad took it better than I anticipated. I wasn't trying to get one over on him. I just wanted to stand on my own two feet—not on his toes if I could help it. Maybe he sensed that: he said fine to no overtime and that we'd talk about the finances. I sensed he felt angry and proud at the same time."

Previously, John had assumed it was either-or. Either he exercised his power or he tended to the relationship. Fearing his father's disapproval, he withheld his power—for years. He accommodated and avoided. What he learned when he said No to his father was that it is possible to use your power *and* at the same time to preserve your relationship. That is the heart of what it means to say a Positive No.

A Positive No Is a "Yes! No. Yes?"

In contrast to an ordinary No which begins with No and ends with No, a Positive No begins with Yes and ends with Yes.

Saying No means, first of all, saying *Yes!* to yourself and protecting what is important to you. As John described his core motivation: "I didn't do it to get a particular response, although

I still cared about what he thought. I did it because *I* thought, *If you don't speak up now, you'll have no self-respect!*" The way John expressed his opening Yes to his father was: "Dad, my family needs me and I intend to spend the holidays with them."

John then followed through with a matter-of-fact *No* that set a clear limit: "I will not be working during weekends and holidays."

He ended with a *Yes?*—an invitation to the other to reach an agreement that respected his needs. "What I propose is that we find a new arrangement that gets the necessary work done in the office while I spend the time I need with my family."

A Positive No, in short, is a *Yes! No. Yes?* The first Yes expresses your *interests,* the No asserts your *power,* and the second Yes furthers your *relationship.* A Positive No thus balances power and relationship in the service of your interests.

Note the distinction between the first Yes and the second Yes. The first Yes is *internally* focused—an affirmation of your interests; the second Yes is *externally* focused—an *invitation* to the other to come to an agreement that satisfies those interests.

The key to a Positive No is respect. What distinguishes a Positive No from accommodation is that you give respect to yourself and what is important for you. What distinguishes a Positive No from an attack is that you give respect to the other too as you say No to their demand or behavior. The Positive No works because as, in John's words, you *stand on your feet, not on their toes.*

A Positive No can best be compared to a tree. The trunk is like your No—straight and strong. But just as a trunk is only the middle part of a tree, so your No is only the middle part of a Positive No. The roots from which the trunk emerges are your first Yes—a Yes to the deeper interests that sustain you. The branches and foliage that reach out from the trunk are your second Yes—a Yes that reaches out toward a possible agreement or relationship. The fruit is the positive outcome you seek.

When it comes to standing up for ourselves, we can learn a lot from trees. They know how to stand tall. They know how to sink their roots deep while reaching for the sky. "Great rooted blossomer" is how the poet William Butler Yeats once described a chestnut tree. That is a Positive No—a strong trunk-like No rooted in a *deeper* Yes and blossoming into a *broader* Yes.

The Three Great Gifts of a Positive No

According to the sages of ancient India, there are three fundamental processes at work in the universe: creation, preservation, and transformation. Saying No is essential to all three processes. If you can learn how to say No skillfully and wisely, you can *create* what you want, *protect* what you value, and *change* what doesn't work. These are the three great gifts of a Positive No.

Create What You Want

Every day, each of us is faced with choices, small and large, where saying Yes to one choice means having to say No to others. Only by saying No to competing demands for your time and energy can you create space for the Yeses in your life, the people and activities that really matter the most to you. Here is the paradoxical secret: *you cannot truly say Yes until you can truly say No.*

I learned this lesson early on in my career from the well-known and extraordinarily successful investor Warren Buffett. Over breakfast one day, he confided in me that the secret to creating his fortune lay in his ability to say No. "I sit there all day and look at investment proposals. I say No, No, No, No, No, No—until I see one that is *exactly* what I am looking for. And then I say Yes. All I have to do is say Yes a few times in my life and I've made my fortune." *Every important Yes requires a thousand Nos.*

No is the key word in defining your strategic focus. Take the example of Southwest Airlines, the most successful airline in the United States and the original model for low-cost airlines worldwide. Its secret, if you think about it, is to deliver a Positive No to its customers. In order to say Yes to success and profitability (the first Yes), its strategy is to say No to reserved seats, No to hot meals, and No to interairline baggage transfers. Saying No to these three services, previously considered essential passenger benefits, enables Southwest to organize its planes for an incredibly quick turnaround at airports. This in turn allows Southwest to say Yes (the second Yes) to affordable fares and to a convenient schedule with reliable frequent flights—the qualities most valued by its customers.

Protect What You Value

Think for a moment about all that matters to you: your personal happiness, the safety of your loved ones, your organization's success, your country's security and sound economic base. Almost everything we care about can be affected or threatened by the behavior of others. A Positive No enables us to set, maintain, and defend the key boundaries—personal, organizational, and societal—that are essential to protecting what we value.

Consider how one group of mothers said No to a seemingly unstoppable epidemic of teenage violence among gangs in their neighborhood in Los Angeles. Feeling utterly helpless at first, the women found strength in prayer and sallied out from church one evening into the streets, where they engaged the teenagers who were waiting for a fight to start. The women talked with their sons and nephews, offered them soda and cookies, and listened to their grievances. Surprised, the young men did not fight that night. So the mothers walked out the next night and the next and the next. Responding to the young men's concerns, they started a few small businesses and offered jobs to the youth as well as conflict resolution training. The violence in the neighborhood greatly abated. The mothers' secret was a Positive No. Their first Yes was to peace and safety, their No was to violence, and their second Yes was to helping the young men find jobs and build their self-respect.

Change What No Longer Works

Whether you are talking about making an organizational change at work, a personal change at home, or a political or economic change at a societal level, every creative change begins with an intentional No to the status quo. Your No might be to complacency and stagnation in the workplace, to dishonesty and abuse in family life, or to injustice and inequity in the larger society.

One family had a son who was destroying his life and his family's life through an addiction to gambling. So the parents and the siblings all got together one day in what is known as an "intervention" and constructively confronted the son. They began by telling him how much he meant to each of them (their first Yes) and then proceeded to tell him that he needed to stop gambling (their No) or lose their support. They invited him to seek help at a residential treatment program for gamblers (their second Yes). Faced with this Positive No, he agreed, got therapeutic help, and recovered from his addiction.

In addition to helping you say No to others, the Positive No method can help you say No to yourself. Almost everyone at times faces the challenge of saying No to temptations and to self-destructive behaviors such as excessive eating, drinking, or consuming. Often we respond by accommodating these temptations, or we attack them with self-judgment, or we simply remain in denial (avoidance) about what is going on inside us. Learning to deliver a Positive No to ourselves—protecting our higher interests while showing respect and empathy for ourselves—can be an invaluable aid in changing ourselves for the better.

How to Use This Book

The Positive No method is what I call uncommon sense: something we intuitively understand but too rarely practice because it goes against our normal impulses and reactions when we want to say No. This book organizes this uncommon sense in a practical framework anyone can use to stand up for themselves without spoiling their valued relationships.

You will find this book organized in three parts or stages. The first describes how to *prepare* a Positive No. The second explains how to *deliver* a Positive No. And the third shows how to *follow through*, turning the other's resistance to your No into acceptance. Each of these three stages is essential to your success.

In this book, you will find that each of these stages has three chapters devoted to it—the first focused on your underlying

Yes, the second on your No to the other's demand or behavior, and the third on your Yes to a positive outcome.

First you *prepare* your Positive No—you uncover your Yes, empower your No, and respect your way to Yes. Then you *deliver* your Positive No—you express your Yes, assert your No, and propose a Yes. Finally, and most important, you *follow through* on your Positive No—you stay true to your Yes, underscore your No, and negotiate to Yes.

I believe that you will obtain more value from reading this book if you keep in mind at least one challenging situation from your life in which you would like to say No. As the chapters lead you step by step through the Positive No process, I encourage you to apply the process to your situation and use it to help you develop an effective strategy.

Saying No is a human dilemma each of us faces at home, at work, and in the world. Everything you care about—your happiness and the well-being of your family, your success in your job, and the health of the larger community—hinges on your ability to say No when it counts. It can be challenging, but the Positive No process makes it easier because it offers a way to stand up for yourself without harming your relationships. No matter how difficult saying No may be for you, you can learn to carry out this simple three-step process and improve your skills with a little practice, patience, and effort. Indeed, the more familiar you become with the process, the more it will become second nature for you.

Once you have mastered the art of the Positive No, it can bring you perhaps the greatest gift of all: the freedom to be who you truly are and to do what you are truly here to do.

PREPARE

3. RESPECT YOUR WAY TO YES

2. EMPOWER YOUR NO

1. UNCOVER YOUR YES

Chapter One

UNCOVER YOUR YES

"In creating, the only hard thing's to begin; a grass-blade's no easier to make than an oak."

—*James Russell Lowell*

Perhaps the single biggest mistake we make when we say No is to *start* from No. We derive our No from what we are *against*—the other's demand or behavior. A Positive No calls on us to do the exact opposite and base our No on what we are *for*. Instead of starting from No, start from Yes. Root your No in a deeper Yes—a Yes to your core interests and to what truly matters.

Nowhere did I learn this more clearly than from a relative of mine who suffered from a serious addiction to alcohol that nearly cost him and others their lives in a car accident. He tried many times to give up the habit but always failed. Then at the age of sixty, just when all hope seemed lost, he found in himself the will to say No and stop drinking. The secret? "When my first grandchild was born," he says, "I wanted more than anything to live long enough to see him grow up. It was his birth that motivated me to get treatment and stop drinking. Since then, for over fifteen years now, I have not touched a drop." His Yes to being present for his grandchildren—to be able to play with them and see them grow—motivated his powerful No to alcohol.

His story serves to illustrate an everyday paradoxical truth: the power of your No comes directly from the power of your Yes.

Your Yes is the underlying purpose for which you are saying No. The first step in the method is to uncover the Yes that lies behind your No. The deeper you go into your core motivation, the more powerful your Yes will be and thus the more powerful your No.

From Reactive to Proactive

The biggest obstacle to saying No successfully is not the other, however difficult they might be. It is ourselves. It is our all-too-human tendency to react—to act with intense emotion but without clear purpose. We humans are reaction machines. And our Nos tend to be reactive. We accommodate out of fear and guilt. We attack out of anger. We avoid out of fear. To get ourselves out of this three-A trap, we need to become proactive, forward-looking, and purposeful.

This challenge is vividly captured in an old Japanese story about a samurai and a fisherman. One day, the samurai went to collect a debt from the fisherman. "I'm sorry," the fisherman said, "but this last year has been a very bad one for me, and I regret to say I do not have the money to repay you." Quick to anger, the samurai drew his sword and prepared to kill the fisherman on the spot. Thinking fast, the fisherman boldly said, "I have been studying martial arts and my master teaches that you should never strike out of anger."

The samurai looked at him for a minute, then slowly lowered his sword. "Your master is wise," he said quietly. "My master used to teach the same lesson. Sometimes my anger gets the better of me. I will give you one more year to repay your debt, but if you fail by even a penny, I will surely kill you."

The samurai returned to his house, arriving late at night. He crept in quietly, not wishing to wake his wife, but to his shock, he found two people in the bed, his wife and a stranger dressed in samurai clothing. With a surge of jealousy and anger, he raised his sword to slay them both, but suddenly the fisherman's words came back to him: "Do not strike out of anger." The samurai stopped for a moment, took a deep breath, and then deliberately made a loud noise. His wife instantly woke up, as did the "stranger," who turned out to be his mother.

"What is the meaning of this?" he yelled. "I almost killed you both!"

"We were afraid of robbers," his wife explained. "So I dressed your mother up in your samurai clothes to scare them off."

A year passed and the fisherman came to see the samurai. "I had an excellent year, so here is your money back and with interest," the fisherman said happily to him.

"Keep your money," replied the samurai. "You repaid your debt long ago."

When you want to say No, remember the samurai's lesson: do not react out of anger—or indeed out of any negative emotion such as fear or guilt. Take a deep breath and focus on your purpose—your Yes—in this situation. Ask yourself what you really want and what is really important here. In other words, shift from being reactive and focused on No, to being proactive and focused on Yes.

This chapter outlines a process that can help you. As the samurai did, you start by stopping and collecting your wits. You then proceed to ask yourself *why*. Why do you want to say No? What are your underlying interests, needs, and values? Once you have answered this question, you can then crystallize your *Yes!*—your intention to protect what matters most to you.

Stop: Go to the Balcony

We do not have a chance of being able to influence the other unless we are first able to control our own natural reactions and emotions.

When we want to say No to an offensive behavior or inappropriate demand, it is only natural to feel angry. But anger can blind us. In the rush to say No, angrily and sometimes vengefully, it is all too easy to lose sight of the prize—advancing our interests. Fear too can prevent us from pursuing our objectives. We imagine in advance the other's reaction to our No. What will they think of us or do to us? What will happen to our relationship, to the deal, and thus to our interests? Paralyzed, we accommodate, giving up on our needs. Guilt has a similar effect. "Who am I to say No?" "I don't deserve the time to myself." "Their needs are more important than mine."

Anger can blind, fear can paralyze, and guilt can weaken.

The first challenge we face, therefore, is internal. Recall the example of the man who said No to his domineering father, who was also his boss. In John's own words, "I didn't stand up to my *dad,* I stood up to my *fears!*" As John recognized, the real obstacle to getting what he wanted was not his father; it was his own fears. "All the action was basically over by the time I spoke to him." That is the key point. *The real action of standing up for yourself takes place inside you before you say No.*

This internal action starts with stopping. Stopping is all-important because it interrupts your natural reaction, buys you time to think, and thus allows you to uncover your Yes. You may stop for a second, an hour, a day, or however long is required. What matters is to stop and get some perspective on the situation before proceeding with your No.

I like to use the metaphor of "going to the balcony." The balcony is a detached state of mind you can access anytime you choose. Imagine yourself for a moment as an actor on a stage about to speak your lines—your No. Now picture yourself up on a balcony overlooking the stage, a place where you can see the scene clearly from afar. The balcony is a place of perspective, calm, and clarity. From a balcony perspective, it is much easier to uncover the Yes behind your No.

I came to truly appreciate this lesson when I was asked to facilitate a difficult discussion in the mid-1990s between Russian and Chechen leaders about how to end the tragic war in Chechnya. This discussion took place at the Peace Palace in The Hague in the very same conference room used for the international tribunal on war crimes in the former Yugoslavia. The Chechen vice president began his long speech by making a series of vociferous accusations against the Russians, saying they should stay in that room because they themselves would soon be on trial for war crimes. He then turned to me and, looking me right in the eye, began attacking: "You Americans have been supporting the Russians in their war crimes! And, what is more, you are violating the rights of self-determination of the people of Puerto Rico!" As he went on with his accusations, others around the table looked at me to see how I would respond. Would I say No to the round of accusations?

I felt defensive and distracted, thinking, "I don't like the turn this conversation is taking. Why is he attacking *me*? I'm just trying to help. Puerto Rico? What do I know about Puerto Rico?" I felt reactive. Should I just accept this treatment? Should I respond in kind? Should I say nothing at all?

Fortunately, the translation time gave me a chance to go to the balcony. I took a deep breath and tried to calm myself. Our purpose, I remembered, was to try to bring peace to the people in Chechnya and Russia. That was my Yes. On that basis, I was ready to say No to this vein of accusation that would lead us nowhere.

When my turn came to respond, I simply said to the Chechen vice president, "I hear your criticism of my country and I take it as a sign that we are among friends and can speak candidly with each other. I know your people have suffered terribly. What we are here to do is to find a way to stop the suffering and bloodshed in Chechnya. Let us try to come up with some practical steps that can be taken today." The discussion got back on track. Going to the balcony enabled me to uncover my Yes.

Take a Time-Out

These days the scarcest resource is time to think. Look for opportunities to go to the balcony whenever possible so that you can reflect on your Yes.

When you want to take a time-out, rote phrases can come in handy. If the other is making an unwanted demand, for instance, you could say:

- "I'm sorry, but this is not a good time to talk about this. Let's talk about it this afternoon."
- "Let me think about it and I'll get back to you tomorrow."
- "I need to consult my partner."
- "Let me make a phone call to check something first."

If the other is behaving offensively, you could use a phrase like:

- "Why don't we take a break?"
- "Time-out for five minutes."
- "Would you excuse me? I need a coffee refill."

Achok, a Tibetan friend of mine, once told me: " 'Yes' and 'No' are very important phrases, but another phrase that is really important sometimes is 'wait a minute.' Sometimes you don't know whether to say Yes or No. So the best answer is 'wait a minute,' which gives you the time to decide." Achok was right. Before saying No, it is often wise to wait a minute.

During the time-out, step out of the room for a moment. Use the moment of quiet to think or consult with a colleague. Imagine it is a customer pressing you for what you fear may be an unrealistic delivery date. In his presence, you might be inclined to agree but, after talking with your colleague on the phone, you realize this would be a big mistake. Giving yourself a chance to reflect before responding can make all the difference between a reactive Yes and a proactive No.

If you are feeling angry or fearful, go for a walk or engage in your favorite form of exercise. Getting your muscles working and your heart pumping can help discharge anger and reduce fear so when you do say No, you can say it from a place of calm and balance.

Listen to Your Emotions

What causes us to react are our negative emotions. Fear and guilt drive us to accommodate or avoid, while anger drives us to attack. Acting out our emotions only gets in the way of our being able to pursue our purpose. Yet suppressing our emotions does not work either. Rather than making our feelings disappear, suppression merely drives them underground, from where they leak out at inopportune moments.

Fortunately, there is a third way to deal with our emotions, far less dramatic than acting them out and far less stressful than suppressing them. *Become aware of your emotions* and, in so doing, take control of them rather than let them take control of you. The most effective way to deal with your negative emotions is not to *act* them out. It is to *hear* them out.

Consider the example of a friend of mine who was having great difficulties persuading her three-year-old daughter to go to preschool. Whenever the time would come to go to school, the daughter would throw a fit and make a scene, insisting on staying home. The mother did not know how to say No effectively. Feeling anguished, fearful, guilty, angry, and frustrated all at once, she would seesaw between hard-edged insistence (attack) and giving in to her daughter's tantrums (accommodate).

One day, the mother took a different tack. She took time to prepare her No, talking with a close friend about her feelings. With her friend's help, she was able to trace her anxiety back to her own need for love and belonging. She came to realize that her anxiety around sending her child to school came from her own childhood feelings of abandonment by *her* mother. Since she knew that she loved her daughter and that sending her to school was not a form of abandonment, she was able to relax and let go of the anxiety she was feeling. The next day, she simply said No to her daughter's insistence on staying home: "You are going to school today." No hesitation, no edge, just a matter-of-fact announcement. To her surprise, there was no resistance and no scene. Her daughter went to school quietly and willingly.

As you trace your emotions back to your underlying needs, a subtle transformation can take place, as it did for my friend. Once you have truly understood the hidden message of your emotions, once they have delivered their message and accomplished their mission, their intensity usually subsides and you grow calmer, more centered, and more effective. Once you have truly heard out your feelings, you do not need to act them out.

So begin by naming your fear or anger or guilt. Recognize them as natural reactions to the other's demand or behavior. Listen to them the way you would listen to a good friend. Let them express themselves fully to you.

Observe your emotions almost as if you were a neutral witness: "I *notice* some feelings of anger inside of me." You are not being cold and distant, just studying your emotions with interest and concern as a friend might. It may help to describe them to a friend or to write them down in a journal.

Think of yourself as "having" or "experiencing" your emotions rather than "being" them. Consider the difference between "I *am* angry" and "I *have* a feeling of anger inside me." The first identifies you directly as your emotion; it sounds almost as if that is all you are. When you *are* your emotions, you may naturally be impelled to act them out. In contrast, the language of "have" allows you to experience the emotions without feeling possessed by them. *You* have the emotions; *they* don't have you.

Keep Asking Yourself Why

Once you are on the balcony and in control of your emotions, you can now proceed to uncover the underlying motivations for your No. A simple but powerful technique is to keep asking yourself the magical question "Why?"

Uncover Your Interests

No is a position, a concrete stance, a statement of what you do not want. Interests, by contrast, are the wants, desires, aspirations, and concerns underlying the No. If your position is No to your co-worker's smoking in the office, for example, your interests may be a desire for fresh, clean air and a need for healthy lungs. Interests are the silent movers and drivers behind positions. Interests, in other words, are what you would like to say Yes to.

Think for a moment of what exactly you would like to say No to. What is the demand or request you would like to refuse? What is the behavior you find inappropriate or offensive? Picture this in your mind—be very concrete and specific.

Now ask yourself what Yes lies behind your No. The answer isn't always obvious. While we usually know our position, often we haven't probed for our underlying interests.

I remember one mediation process in which I spent a few days with the commanders of a separatist movement who had been fighting for twenty-five years for the independence of their people. They had, in other words, been issuing a very loud and violent No. My first question for them was: "I understand your *position*: independence. But tell me about your *interests*. In other words, *why* do you want independence? What underlying interests are you hoping independence will satisfy?" There ensued a long silence and then a somewhat awkward struggle to answer the question.

The commanders knew their *position*. It was crystal clear. But the truth was that they could not fully articulate their interests. Was their chief interest economic—a fair share of the region's rich natural resources? Was it political—the ability to run their own affairs and elect their own parliament? Was it security—the ability to defend their people against physical threats to their lives and well-being? What did they really want and in what order of priority? Here they had been fighting for years, at the cost of thousands of lives, yet they had not systematically thought through *why* they were really fighting.

Digging beneath your position to understand your interests, and asking "Why?" again and again, is not merely an academic exercise. It is hard to satisfy your real interests if you are not sure what they are. The commanders, as they readily acknowledged, were unlikely anytime soon to obtain their position of independence through military means. In the medium term, however, they had the opportunity to advance their interests in recognition, self-rule, and control over their economic resources through an agreement on democratic elections, which they were confident they would win. Local political control in turn might move them further toward their long-term goal of independence. Uncovering the interests underlying their position helped lead them, eventually, over a period of years, into an unexpected peace agreement with their adversaries.

It is essential to keep asking the *why* question because the fuel needed to be able to say No effectively comes ultimately not from your position but from what lies behind your position: your underlying interests, your Yes.

Remembering the three great gifts of No can help you discern your interests. Ask yourself:

• What am I seeking to *create* by saying No? What other activity or person am I wanting to say Yes to?

• What am I seeking to *protect* by saying No? What core interest of mine is at risk if I say Yes or simply continue to accept the other's behavior?

• What am I seeking to *change* by saying No? What is wrong with the other's current behavior (or the situation) and what would be improved if that behavior (or situation) changed?

Uncover Your Needs

It is useful to probe even deeper into your underlying motivation. Often, when we list our interests, we are really listing our *wants*—our everyday desires, aspirations, and concerns. These are the things or conditions we would like to have, often very much. We want our office to be comfortable, the deal to be profitable, the vacation to be relaxing, and the price to be affordable. If we probe deeper, we will find underneath these wants a set of core motivations—our *needs*.

Needs are the basic drives that motivate human behavior. Perhaps the five most common basic human needs are:

• Safety or survival
• Food, drink, and other life necessities

- Belonging and love
- Respect and meaning
- Freedom and control over one's fate

Basic human needs underlie everyday behavior. Imagine your boss has asked you to work for the third weekend in a row, and you want to say No because you and your spouse have long-standing plans to go away. Your interests, as you first think about it, are to get away, to be able to keep your plans, and not to feel overworked. But to get at the underlying basic needs, you need to keep asking yourself why you *really* want to say No. Beneath the interest in getting away is an interest in strengthening your marriage, and beneath that, if you dig deeper, is a basic need for belonging and love. Beneath the interest in keeping your plans is the basic need for autonomy and control over your fate. Beneath the feeling of resentment at being overworked by your boss is a basic need for respect.

A sales manager, a participant in one of my seminars, was having trouble saying No to his biggest customer, who was continually pressing him for more and more price reductions. "What is your underlying Yes?" I asked him.

"Maintaining a steady stream of revenue," he replied.

"But why?" I pressed him.

"Profit," he said.

"But *why* do you want profits?" I asked again.

"So we can all work," he said, gesturing at his colleagues, "and so I can put food on my family's table." It boiled down to this basic need. The sales manager's No to his customer's demands became more powerful because it was rooted in something he cared deeply about.

It pays to dig deep in uncovering your needs. The deeper you go, the more likely you are to hit bedrock, a place of strength and stability that can anchor your No.

To uncover your needs, listen to your emotions. Emotions

have intelligence—they are the language used by your core needs to signal that they are not being met. Fear alerts us to possible threat. Anger tells us that something in the situation is wrong and may need to be corrected. Guilt alerts us to be sensitive to important relationships. Gut feelings can warn us that a deal we are about to sign ought to be reconsidered. If we can listen to these feelings rather than react to them, we can benefit greatly.

That certainly has been my own experience. I have learned to listen to my gut feelings when I am faced with an important decision such as whether to accept a major work engagement. I have found that those gut feelings are almost inevitably correct, pointing to needs that I haven't properly addressed. If I get a queasy feeling about accepting a new project, for example, it usually means I am overlooking my need for more family or personal time.

Treat your emotions as signposts, pointing at your core needs. Rather than being your enemy, your emotions can become your ally, for they can help you uncover your Yes.

Uncover Your Values

Alongside the needs that drive you are the values that motivate you. Values are the principles and beliefs that guide your life. They are evoked by such phrases as "Always act with integrity" or "Treat everyone fairly." While values vary from culture to culture and from individual to individual, certain values are widely held in common around the world, including honesty, integrity, respect, tolerance, kindness, solidarity, fairness, courage, and peace.

Values can provide strong motivation for you to be able to say No. It is often easier for people to take a stand on behalf of something larger than themselves than it is to take a stand for their own personal needs.

Recall the story of Sherron Watkins, the Enron employee who had the courage to write a memo to her boss, CEO Kenneth Lay, expressing her strong concern about the unethical and illegal accounting practices then taking place at Enron, and warning that the company "could implode in a wave of accounting scandals." Tragically, her memo went unheeded and the giant energy corporation fell into bankruptcy and criminal investigation, causing thousands of unsuspecting employees to lose their jobs and life's savings. While her memo did not save Enron, her courageous action of standing up for what was right was given widespread publicity; she was named one of *Time* magazine's people of the year, and held up as a role model that will surely encourage others to do what they can to prevent future Enrons.

In saying No to illegal and unethical accounting practices at Enron, Sherron Watkins was saying Yes to her values of honesty and integrity. Even though Watkins expected to be fired for her memo, "there was no option about whether or not she was going to send it. She knew she had to say something," her mother later told the *Washington Post*. It was a question of values. As Sherron Watkins' story suggests, uncovering your underlying values can provide the motivation necessary to deliver a powerful and positive No.

Reach Down to Your Core

As you uncover your needs and values, it is useful to ask yourself the question: "What really matters?" What are your true priorities?

The prospect of saying No often triggers self-doubt and anxiety. You find yourself asking, "Can I actually do it, and if I say No, will I be able to stick to it?" To counter your inner critic, it is essential to dig deep down to your core, your true self, that place of inner certainty and conviction. Just as John, in the example described in the Introduction, dug deep to find the self-respect that allowed him to stand up to his father, so you too can reach down to the core of self-respect that will enable you to stand up and say No.

Keep probing. What is your deeper purpose? What is true and right for you? What is the message from your heart and soul?

One senior manager I know was offered a tempting promotion at work, but it would mean a lot of travel away from home. "I have small children," he told me. "So, even though the opportunity was very difficult to pass up, I said No." He said No in order to say Yes to being with his children. His children were what mattered to him most. Fortunately, not long afterward he was offered another job that allowed him to work close to home.

This exercise applies not only to individuals but also to leaders of organizations or nations who must discern their true priorities. This was the challenge faced by James Burke, chairman of the pharmaceutical company Johnson & Johnson, when he learned that one child and six adults in the Chicago area had died of poisoning from ingesting Tylenol. Apparently someone had laced the capsules with deadly cyanide and then put them back on the store shelves. Tylenol was the company's most profitable product, commanding 35 percent of the market in over-the-counter painkillers. The question arose of whether to order a nationwide recall. Many experts inside and outside the company cautioned against it, arguing that the incidents were limited to the Chicago area and that the poisoning was not Johnson & Johnson's fault. But Burke and his colleagues knew exactly what to do. They ordered the entire supply of the product withdrawn from the shelves of pharmacies and drugstores and, furthermore, offered to exchange all of the existing Tylenol capsules in people's homes for Tylenol tablets. This one decision, taken almost immediately, cost the company tens of millions of dollars. In effect, the company said No to continuing to sell Tylenol until they were absolutely confident they could guarantee their customers' safety.

Where did this courageous and enlightened No come from? As Burke and his colleagues explained later, it came directly from consulting the company's credo, written forty years earlier by its visionary president Robert Wood Johnson: "We believe our first responsibility is to the doctors, nurses, and patients, to mothers and fathers and all those who use our products and services." Profits were important, of course, but they came second to the customers' health and safety. Knowing and believing in these core values, everyone in the company knew what to do and instantly got behind the recall decision.

The result? Contrary to conventional wisdom, which held that there was no way the Tylenol brand could recover from the disaster, Tylenol was relaunched within months under the same name in a new tamper-resistant bottle and proceeded to achieve an astonishing recovery in sales and market share. What could easily have turned into a disaster in public confidence for Johnson & Johnson became a confirmation in the public's eyes of the company's integrity and credibility.

So when you are about to say No, it pays to follow the example of James Burke and consult your basic mission and core values. What do you and your organization truly stand for? Think not just of your short-term interest and immediate desires, but of your long-term interest as well. Think not just of your narrow self-interest but also of your enlightened self-interest. It serves us well to listen, as Burke and his colleagues did, to "the better angels of our nature," in Abraham Lincoln's famous phrase.

The goal is to find the deepest source of your No and connect with it. The deeper you go into your Yes, the stronger your No will be.

Crystallize Your Yes!

Now that you have uncovered your deepest interests, needs, and values, you can distill them into a powerful *Yes!* Your *Yes!* is your *intention* to protect and advance your core interests. Needs and values are where you come from; intention is where you want to go. Intention adds to your interests the element of commitment. You don't just have the interest; you make a commitment to fulfilling it. "True strength does not come from physical capacity," declared Mahatma Gandhi. "It comes from an indomitable will." Few things in life are as strong as a clear intention.

The most powerful intentions are positive. They are *for*, not *against*. Think of Nelson Mandela, who spent over forty years fighting the racist system of apartheid in South Africa. The title of his autobiography makes clear what positive intention kept him going through decades of hard struggle and imprisonment. He chose to call his memoir not *Long Walk Away from Apartheid* but rather *Long Walk to Freedom*. His most essential commitment was not *against* apartheid but rather *for* freedom—freedom for himself, for his people, and even for his adversaries.

Distill a Single Intention

Your intention is not something you invent but rather something you crystallize from your interests, needs, and values. What can give real power to your No is to distill all your varied motivations into a single, concentrated intention—your *Yes!*

Uncovering your interests, needs, and values is a divergent activity in which you go from a single position of No to many possible motivations behind it. Creating a single intention is a convergent activity in which you go from many motivations to one intention that sums them all up. If your interests are like the roots of the tree, the base of the trunk where all the roots converge is like your intention.

Begin by making a list of the interests that are motivating you to want to say No and then try to sum them up in a single phrase that best captures their essence. For John, the man who said No to his domineering father, that phrase was "self-respect." For my relative who said No to his alcoholism, that phrase was "being with my grandchildren." Ask yourself: "What am I truly standing up for? What overriding value or need am I protecting? Is it my happiness, my family's well-being, my company's brand, my personal integrity, or is it something else?"

For a senior executive of a prominent international hotel chain, the Yes was to his brand. He faced the challenge of saying No to the powerful owner of a Caribbean resort hotel within the chain who was demanding exceptions to the brand standards as construction on the new hotel neared completion. The executive said No, not as a matter of mere policy but because he realized that the brand was the company's main asset. "Our brand means nothing if we do not adhere to our standards," he later explained to me. Having uncovered and crystallized his Yes, he did not find it hard to say No to the owner, saying that "The reason why you and others want our brand on your hotel is that we do not make exceptions on matters of quality."

Since your intention is often general, it is helpful to give it specificity by envisioning a positive outcome that would fulfill your intention. Ask yourself: "What kind of concrete solution would satisfy my interests?" Use your mind's eye to visualize the outcome you aspire to, just as athletes often do before a competition. Exactly what would it look like if the other agreed to respect your needs? This kind of concrete visualization can help give you the confidence and conviction you need to succeed.

It also helps to write down your intention and even announce it to a colleague or a friend. It will remind you of your commitment to yourself.

Distinguish Between *Whether* and *How*

Sometimes we may find ourselves thinking, "I would like to say No, but there's no way I can imagine saying No to my mother, boss, or friend." We sabotage our intention to say No even before we speak with the other.

"I don't see how I can say No," you may say to yourself when good friends ask you to help them move. You know you don't have the time right now, but your mind floods with so much guilt and fear that it just seems inconceivable to say No. So you give in and say OK. Afterward, the regret, resentment, and anger set in—because saying Yes was the last thing you wanted to do at that point.

For many of us, this happens every day. And it springs from the common practice of mixing up *whether* to do something with *how* to do it. We confuse the question of whether or not we will say No with the question of how we will say No. Since the *how* seems impossible, the *whether* seems predetermined. In fact, to make ourselves feel better, we rationalize to ourselves, "It's OK with me. I didn't really need the time to myself anyway."

There is an alternative, however. It is to distinguish in your own decision-making process between the *whether* and the *how*. Clarify your true intention first as you consider what you really want to do in this situation. Once the question of *whether* is resolved, then you can consider the *how*, which may turn out to be easier than your fears would lead you to believe.

Turn Your Emotions into Resolve

Once you have clarified your intention, it is time to give it energy. That energy can come from your emotions, properly harnessed.

In addition to serving as warning signals of unmet needs, emotions play another critical function: they provide fuel for action. They impel us to take appropriate action to protect our core interests, giving us courage and resolve. As champion athletes know well, emotions, if directed properly, can provide enormous motivational power.

So instead of letting your emotions drive you, harness them and channel them into resolve—the will to address your unmet needs and advance your deepest values. Your positive intention does not come out of a vacuum, but rather *grows* out of your emotions.

No one understood and demonstrated this process of transformation better than Mahatma Gandhi, who, without a single weapon or man under arms, succeeded in putting an end to the centuries-long colonial domination of India by the British Empire. He explained his secret as follows: "I had learned through bitter experience the one supreme lesson to conserve my anger, and as heat is transmuted into energy, even so our anger controlled can be transmuted into a power which can move the world."

To transform negative emotion into positive intention, first observe and *accept* your emotions, tracing them back to their source in unmet interests and needs. Watch the emotional charge shift from negative to positive as you listen deeply to your feelings. Then, as Gandhi suggested, *conserve* your energy. In other words, refrain from impulsive reaction, which is only a reckless waste of your precious energy. Finally, at the right moment, purposively *release* your emotional energy as resolve. Use it as fuel for appropriate action, not reaction. Let it serve as sustained motivational power for your No.

"Gandhi taught me at age twelve that anger is as useful and powerful as electricity," writes Mahatma Gandhi's grandson Arun, "but only if we use it intelligently. We must learn to respect anger as we do electricity."

In truth, there are no intrinsically negative emotions, only negatively charged emotions, which have the potential to become positively charged. Emotions such as fear and anger can be either destructive or constructive, depending on how you deal with them—as I learned during a very tense public gathering in Venezuela.

At the height of political tensions in Venezuela in 2003, at a time when many international observers feared an outbreak of civil war, I was invited by the United Nations to facilitate a daylong meeting of citizen leaders, including both ardent supporters and bitter opponents of President Hugo Chávez. The meeting was open to anyone, and the venue was an old theater in downtown Caracas seating five hundred people. Close to a thousand people showed up, and the National Guard was called out for fear violence might erupt between partisan groups. Naturally, the atmosphere in the room was charged with fear and tension. After introductions by several high-level international dignitaries, the podium was handed over to me to facilitate the meeting.

Acting on an intuition, I asked the participants to visualize for themselves concrete images of the destructiveness of the conflict—someone they knew who had been wounded or killed, a lost job, a broken friendship or family tie, a child's nightmare, whatever it might be for them. Then I asked them, "What Spanish word would you use to say No to the political violence?" The word several audience members suggested was "*Basta!* Enough!" So I said, "OK, then, I want to ask you a favor.

I would like to hear for one moment the voice of the Venezuelan people, a voice that until now has been silenced, the voice of sanity. Keeping your personal image of the conflict in mind, I would like to ask you to call out together 'Basta' with all the emotion you feel. Will you do this for me?" They nodded. On the count of three, a loud "Basta!" swept the room. It was powerful. I still felt some holding back, perhaps driven by shyness, so I asked them to please repeat it. They did, and it was very strong. I asked them one final time, and with this third "Basta!" the entire theater shook to its rafters.

I mention this story because the atmosphere in the room changed perceptibly at that moment. Without overstating, I would say that the negatively charged emotions of fear and anger shifted into a positively charged intention to help put an end to the destructiveness of the conflict. As if to confirm this, that very afternoon in the theater the participants organized a committee to work together for peace in Venezuela. They met weekly and began to organize dialogues, street theater, radio and TV programs, school programs, and youth dances, all intended to reduce tensions and promote understanding. Three years after the fact, at the time of this writing, they are still going strong. They have grown into a social movement they call Aquí Cabemos Todos, meaning "here we all fit." It is fair to say that they have made a genuine difference in their own lives and that of their country.

Here is the lesson: you can use your emotions to mobilize yourself to say No and stand up for what is important to you. Anxiety, fear, and anger bring you the gift of transformative energy, which is precisely what you need to make internal and external changes. If you are able to hear them out respectfully instead of acting them out destructively, these emotions can become your friends and allies. They can give you the guts to say No—a full-bodied, deep-bellied, strong-voiced No.

Uncover Your Yes

Uncovering your Yes accomplishes three useful tasks:

• *It grounds you in something positive.* You can now stand on your feet without standing on their toes. Your No can be *for* your needs, not *against* the other. Instead of rejecting the other by saying No, you can simply say Yes to what matters most to you.

• *It gives you a sense of direction.* You now know where you are going with your No.

• *It gives you energy.* You now have the fuel to deliver your No and to sustain it in the face of resistance.

Now that you have uncovered your Yes, it is time to empower your No. That is the subject of the next chapter.

Chapter Two

EMPOWER YOUR NO

"To be prepared is half the victory."
—*Miguel de Cervantes Saavedra*

Saying No is not easy. The other may react strongly to your No. You need confidence to stand up for yourself in the face of the other's reaction. You need power to be able to follow through on your No if the other refuses to respect it. Just as critical as uncovering your Yes, therefore, is empowering your No.

Develop Positive Power

Once you have distilled your interests into a clear and strong intention, it is time to back up your intention with a Plan B, a practical strategy that will address your core interests in case the other refuses to accept your No. Plan B is positive power. While negative power is the power to punish the other, positive power is the power to protect and advance your interests and needs.

One person's story can serve to illustrate the enormous potential of positive power. She was born into the family of an oppressed racial minority and worked as a tailor's assistant in a department store. The empowered No she delivered to racial prejudice in her hometown set in motion the civil rights movement in the United States. Her name was Rosa Parks.

At the end of a long workday in December 1955, Parks boarded a city bus to go home. At that time, in a large part of the United States, black people suffered the injustice of legalized segregation in all aspects of social life, including public transportation. They were treated as second-class citizens in a society that professed a commitment to human equality. Parks describes what happened next:

"I did not sit at the very front of the bus; I took a seat with a man who was next to the window—the first seat that was allowed for 'colored' people to sit in. We were not disturbed until we reached the third stop after I boarded the bus. At this point a few white people boarded the bus, and one white man was left standing. When the driver noticed him standing, he spoke to us (the black man and two black women across the aisle) and told us to let the man have the seat. The other three all stood up. But the driver saw me still sitting there. He said would I stand up, and I said, 'No, I will not.' Then he said, 'I'll have you arrested.' And I told him he could do that. So he didn't move the bus any further. Several black people left the bus.

"Two policemen got on the bus in a couple of minutes. The driver told the police that I would not stand up. The policeman walked down and asked me why I didn't stand up, and I said I didn't think I should stand up. 'Why do you push us around?' I asked him. And he said, 'I don't know. But the law is the law and you are under arrest.' As soon as he said that, I stood up and the three of us left the bus together."

Rosa Parks was put in jail. Although she was freed that night on the posting of a bond, her arrest galvanized the black community and triggered an unprecedented eleven-month boycott of the buses, led by a young local pastor by the name of Martin Luther King Jr.

Rosa Parks possessed the two essential ingredients of positive power: a strong intention and a practical Plan B to back it up. Her intention had been shared and refined during years of activism. In the popular retelling of the story, her refusal to give up her seat is often portrayed as the spontaneous action of a tired seamstress. In fact, Parks was an experienced and educated activist of strong beliefs, a long-term member of the local chapter of the NAACP, a national organization working for equal treatment for black people. The chapter's leaders had long been looking for a test case to challenge the legality of segregated bus seating and to win over public opinion with a series of protests. When the opportunity presented itself, Parks and her colleagues were ready with their Plan B.

A friend once described Parks as someone who, as a rule, did not defy authority but, once determined on a course of action, refused to back down: "She might ignore you, go around you, but never retreat." Parks was perfectly prepared to face the consequences of arrest and ready to take her legal case all the way to the Supreme Court if necessary. In the end, that is exactly what happened. The Supreme Court eventually ruled against segregation on public transportation, and the rest is history.

Parks' Plan B was intended not to punish anyone but rather to protect the deeper Yes behind her No, a Yes to dignity and equality for all. Even though she appeared to have little objective power in the situation on the bus, she had positive power to back up her No and support her Yes, and that was sufficient to trigger a revolution for human dignity that reverberated throughout the nation and, indeed, the world.

Turn Fear into Confidence

When faced with the task of devising a Plan B, many people resist, reluctant to engage in "worst-case thinking." They may think that it is unnecessary or disloyal, or that they can do it later. In my experience, however, there is no more critical and ultimately effective exercise for you to undertake if you are to deliver a powerful No. For in addition to the objective power that it gives you, it helps transmute your fear and anger into confidence and resolve. Think of it not as "worst-case thinking" but as planning an alternative means of success.

If you believe you are totally dependent on the other's cooperation, you effectively become a hostage. You naturally feel fearful and angry. The desperation you may feel can easily lead you to accommodate or to attack. Perhaps Plan B's biggest benefit is that it gives you the psychological freedom you need to say No to the other effectively—without accommodating, avoiding, or attacking.

The great irony is that the more you *need* the other to do what you want, the more power you give them over you and the less power you have to influence the situation. In situations of conflict, the other is more likely to do what you would like them to do if you don't *need* them to do it.

Consider a real-life marital dispute. Joan was extremely unhappy about the lack of communication with her husband, whom I will call Jack. She had a strong need for connection and, from her point of view, they rarely if ever really talked. For years, Joan had criticized and nagged him to talk with her, but the more she did, the more he retreated. Her No to his behavior only seemed to provoke the opposite response to what she was seeking. Their marriage was on the verge of disintegrating.

After lengthy counseling, Joan thought hard about her Plan B, which was to separate from her husband, something she did not want to do. Still, she came to terms with this as a real possibility if her core needs could not be met. She gathered her courage and stood up to her fears. She then felt empowered to adopt a different and more confident approach to saying No.

"I'm no longer willing to accept how rarely we talk," she calmly informed her husband, "and I'm no longer willing to push you to do it. But don't assume I'm accepting things the way they are because I won't be nagging or criticizing you anymore. For myself, I don't want to be pathetically grateful just because my partner talks to me.... And for you, I don't want you feeling pressured all the time by a screeching wife. I'll interpret what you do from here on as indicating your decision about how *you* really want to live. I'll make my decision about my life accordingly."

In other words, Joan was not trying to control how her husband would act. She was only choosing how *she* would act. She was committing herself to living a different kind of life, one that would address her needs, *regardless* of how Jack continued to behave. Paradoxically, this approach helped save the marriage and allowed it to deepen, for Joan's newfound confidence and power enabled her to stop her destructive criticism, and Jack responded by opening up and talking more about what he felt and needed. A Positive No made her closer to rather than further from her husband.

The challenge then in saying No is to express the "need"—the interest, desire, or concern—without the "neediness." The neediness creates stress for both of you—a feeling of coercion for the other, of weakness and dependence for you. You may have certain needs, but you don't "need" the other to cooperate. You would very much like them to cooperate, but if not, you have alternative ways to address your needs.

The challenge is to stand up to yourself first, as Joan clearly did—to face your fears about the loss of the relationship or the deal, your fears about what the other might do in reaction or retaliation to your No, and to move on from those fears to taking responsibility for meeting your own interests and needs, with or without the other's cooperation.

Devise a Plan B

Plan B is your best course of action to address your interests *if* the other does not accept your No. It is your capacity to address your needs *independent* of whether or not the other decides to respect your interests. In negotiation language, Plan B is called your BATNA (best alternative to a negotiated agreement). *B* in this sense stands for *BATNA* as well as for *backup*.

If you are saying No to a boss's abusive behavior, your Plan B may be to seek a transfer to another department or to get support from human resources. If you are saying No to a customer who keeps pressing you with unreasonable demands, your Plan B may be to find a new customer, or it may be to involve your boss, who can contact your customer's boss to see if they can work it out. These admittedly may not be attractive alternatives, but they are important for you to keep in mind as you prepare to say No. If the other has more power than you, developing a practical Plan B can help you level the playing field so that you can say No with greater ease.

In my experiences dealing with the medical system on behalf of my daughter, I found it invaluable to have in mind a Plan B. To protect our daughter's well-being, for example, my wife and I needed to set firm limits on repetitive and often traumatic medical exams that were done for the benefit of medical students but that had no genuine benefit for our daughter. If medical staff did not respect these limits after repeated polite requests, our Plan B was to appeal as high within the system as we could and, if necessary, to change doctors and hospitals.

Plan B is an action you can take independent of the other's cooperation. Picturing the Positive No as a journey, imagine a fork in the road. One fork leads to acceptance of your No—call it Plan A, with the *A* standing for *acceptance* or *agreement*. The other fork leads to your Plan B, your backup.

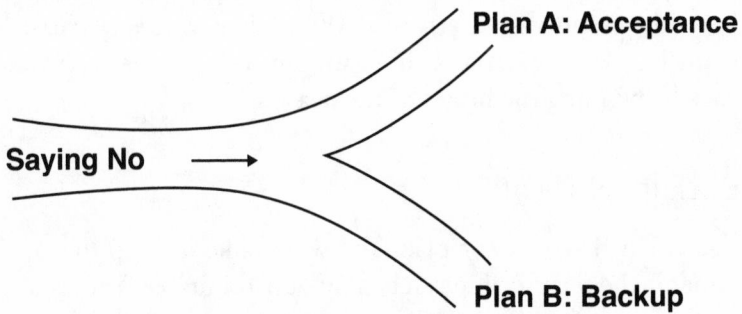

The story of "the man who said No to Wal-Mart" demonstrates the power of a Plan B. Jim Wier was CEO of Simplicity, a company that owned Snapper, a high-quality brand of lawn mowers. Snapper did tens of millions of dollars of business with Wal-Mart. Wal-Mart was insisting on a substantial price reduction and dangling in return the prospect of dramatically increased purchasing. In the business world, it is widely considered suicide to say No to Wal-Mart, and most CEOs would have found this tempting offer impossible to refuse. But not Jim Wier, who had taken a hard look at where this process would lead over ten years: to continual price reductions and the inevitable sacrifice of the quality, reliability, and durability that Snapper stood for in the eyes of its consumers. Even though Wal-Mart represented almost 20 percent of their sales, Wier said No and chose to lose that 20 percent overnight—in order to say Yes to Snapper's core values and, in Wier's view, its long-term survival.

What enabled Wier to make this courageous decision was his Plan B. He had developed a plan to sell Snapper lawn mowers exclusively through an independent dealer network—ten thousand dealers who understood the product, could teach customers how to use it, and could service it if something went wrong. "When we told the dealers that they would no longer find Snapper in Wal-Mart," says Wier, "they were very pleased with that decision. And I think we got most of that business back by winning the hearts of the dealers."

Backup, Not Fallback

Your Plan B is a *backup* plan. You would like to keep the customer if the relationship can be mutually profitable. You would prefer to stay in your job if your boss will give you the respect you deserve. You want to stay in your marriage if it is safe and non-abusive. But if it looks like you're not going to get what you need, your Plan B is your last resort, what you will do if the other does not accept your No.

Plan B is sometimes confused with a fallback option—something that the other could agree to if your No turns out not to be acceptable. But Plan B is *not* a fallback—a compromise or less preferred agreement. Plan B is not an *option* for agreement at all but rather an *alternative* to agreement, a course of action you could pursue *independent* of the other's agreement. Your Plan B if you cannot reach agreement with this customer might be to let this particular sale go and seek another customer. Options require the other's agreement or acceptance in the end. Plan B's do not.

Your Plan B can also be a valuable benchmark that you can use to evaluate any proposal you make as part of your Positive No or any possible agreement you might consider. At any point, you can ask yourself, "Which course of action is more likely to satisfy my interests—accepting this agreement or resorting to my Plan B?"

Empowerment, Not Punishment

Under trying circumstances, many people might think the purpose of their Plan B is to punish the other for their inappropriate behavior. If the other does not agree to respect your interests and needs, if your adult child ignores your request for advance notice before dropping off your granddaughter for babysitting, if your colleague continues to make offensive comments, you will make them pay for it.

But Plan B is not punishment. It is not an outlet for your frustration and anger. Plan B is simply what you are going to do to help make sure your interests are respected *even if* the other does not cooperate. In the case of the adult child who frequently expects babysitting without notice, your Plan B might be to say you are sorry, but you were just going out the door to meet a friend, and then leave the house. In the case of your colleague, your Plan B might be to bring the matter of your colleague's offensive comments to the attention of human resources or others who could persuade him to desist.

Plan B is not so much *power over* the other as it is *power to* meet your own interests. That is what makes it *positive* power.

At this stage of preparing to deliver your Positive No, it is important simply to know that you have a Plan B. We will discuss in Chapter 8 whether and how to mention your Plan B to the other. At this point, develop your Plan B for your own benefit and confidence.

Strengthen Your Plan B

Sometimes we feel at a loss because we can't think of an attractive Plan B. Take this not as a reason for discouragement but as an impetus to improve your Plan B, as the following example illustrates.

A large U.S. company had recently launched a new product in the marketplace. They had hoped for a great success, but the sales were disappointing and competition was stiffer than expected. Knowing that many customers found the price high, the company was trying to cut costs wherever possible. It turned out that the biggest part of the cost was a key ingredient manufactured for them by a company in Europe.

The company asked the supplier to cut its price and offered to send in a team of cost-cutting consultants, but the supplier bristled at the request. "We have been in business for over two hundred years. You've hardly been a country for two hundred years. We don't tell you how to run your business, so don't tell us how to run ours!" The company executives were frustrated but felt they had little leverage, for they had signed a ten-year contract with this supplier on a cost-plus basis, guaranteeing to the supplier reimbursement of all of their costs plus a profit.

The company contacted my colleague Joe Haubenhofer because they wanted help with this difficult negotiation. When Joe met with the company officials to prepare them for the negotiation, they were feeling demoralized and hopeless. How could they stand up for their interests in this situation and, in effect, say No to the supplier's recalcitrant behavior? They felt their hands were tied because they were absolutely dependent on this one supplier. There was nothing they could do. Or so they believed until Joe asked them, "What's your Plan B? What are you going to do if the supplier refuses to cooperate for the rest of the contract?"

"Plan B?" the managers chorused. "That's the problem. We don't have a Plan B! We're locked into this ten-year contract and there is no way out."

"Hold on a minute," Joe replied. "What you mean to say is that your current alternatives—breaking the contract or taking the product off the market—are extremely unattractive. Would you be willing to spend a little time taking a hard look at whether there is any way to improve your Plan B?"

The managers agreed—skeptically, of course. An hour later, in the midst of an intensive brainstorming session, one of them asked, "Is there no other factory in the world that has the technology to make this product?" To which another replied, "Well, as a matter of fact, I seem to remember this plant in the Midwest that may have the necessary technology. But if my memory serves me right, it was closed by its owner."

Someone was dispatched to check out the facts. Later that day, he reported back that the manager had been correct—the plant did have the appropriate technology, and it was closed, but it might be available for sale.

Within a day, the team had drawn up a business plan for purchasing the plant, putting it back into operation, and producing the necessary ingredient in quantity, at the right cost. The plan was presented to senior management and speedily approved as a contingency plan, a Plan B.

Then the team went to work preparing for their upcoming visit to the supplier. It was as if they were a completely different team, my colleague reported. With a satisfactory Plan B in hand, they were no longer demoralized but, on the contrary, confident. They carefully assessed the supplier's interests and perceptions and sought to invent mutually advantageous options for cutting costs and preserving their partnership.

As it turned out, they never had to use their Plan B or even to reveal it. Their careful preparation gave them the confidence they needed to negotiate effectively with the supplier and reach agreement on a strategy for cutting operational costs. And the key factor in this unexpected success, the company negotiators told me later, was that confidence. It enabled them to transform their negatively charged emotions of fear and resignation into resolve and determination.

Brainstorm a Variety of Plans

In developing your Plan B, it is valuable to consider a variety of possible alternatives. The managers in this example began by participating in a brainstorming session and thus came up with a creative alternative that no one had considered before.

The biggest obstacle to coming up with creative alternatives is a little voice in the back of our head that keeps saying, "That won't work!" or "That's ridiculous!" These are phrases that kill off potentially creative ideas. That critical voice comes from the part of the brain that evaluates and judges. While useful and even necessary, it gets in the way of the creative part of the brain that generates new ideas. The whole secret of brainstorming is to separate the two cognitive functions. Invent first, evaluate later.

The golden rule of brainstorming is to suspend all criticism for a certain period of time, whether a few minutes or a few hours. Generate as many ideas as you can. Welcome wild ideas—many of the best plans start off as wild ideas. Then you can start to evaluate, sifting through the ideas and placing an asterisk by the most promising ones.

Brainstorming is often best done with others—friends, colleagues, and associates. Each person's contribution usually stimulates ideas in the others, like a firecracker setting off other firecrackers around it.

Develop one or several possible alternatives into concrete operational plans. This process takes what might otherwise remain a wild idea and turns it into a serious plan that can command respect and support—exactly what the managers did when they researched what sounded like an impossibility (finding another source) and wrote a business plan that could be presented to the company's leaders.

In coming up with alternatives, here are a few different types to consider:

Do it yourself.

One alternative is *unilateral* in nature: What can you do on your own to satisfy your interests and needs? What if you no longer depended on the other? How could you best manage independent of the other's cooperation? The managers in the case discussed above, for example, developed the possibility of manufacturing the needed ingredient independent of the supplier.

Exit.

Another unilateral self-help strategy is exit. What would it mean for you to leave the situation or relationship with the other? Coping with a difficult boss, an employee investigates other job possibilities within the same organization and outside. Faced with saying No to a difficult customer, a salesperson cultivates other customers. A woman being abused by her partner prepares to leave home with her children and take refuge in a family member's house. A lawyer I know was asked to work on a project she found "morally repugnant and offensive." She was able to say No effectively because she had made the decision beforehand "to quit my job if my No was not accepted."

Third side.

There are also *trilateral* alternatives. Are there potential third parties to whom you could turn for help if you cannot reach initial agreement with the other? If a neighbor continues to play loud music, you could ask the building supervisor to intervene or bring the matter up at a building residents' meeting. If you are unable to persuade your co-worker to stop asking the secretary to put your work aside in favor of his, you may need to go to the boss. Or your Plan B might be to use the court system, as Rosa Parks did in taking her case all the way to the Supreme Court.

Intermediate and ultimate plans.

If you cannot reach agreement with the other, your first resort may be not your full Plan B but a smaller intermediate step. You can develop a sequence of plans starting from the smallest and leading up to the ultimate big plan. One restaurant chain, faced with saying No to a restaurant franchisee who was consistently failing to meet the quality standards associated with the brand, prepared an intermediate plan of putting the franchisee on probation. The chain's ultimate Plan B, if the franchisee did not bring their establishment up to standard, was to remove the brand from the franchisee.

Build a Winning Coalition

If the other is more powerful than you, one Plan B you could consider is to build a winning coalition.

In my seminars, I like to use a teaching story about a wise Zen master who in the course of giving a class to a group of students deliberately puts one of them in a quandary. As the student is lifting a cup of tea to his lips, the master says: "If you drink that cup of tea, I will beat you with this stick. And if you *don't* drink that cup of tea, I will beat you with this stick."

"What would you do if you were that student?" I ask the seminar participants.

The most common response I receive is: "I would drink the tea. I might as well enjoy it." Another common response is: "I would throw the tea in the master's face." Those are the two classic responses to superior power: submission because you have no choice and attack. Neither, however, usually proves satisfying.

Then people start to get imaginative with their answers: "I would offer him the tea." "I would ask why." "I would take forever so he couldn't tell whether I was drinking it or not drinking it." And so on.

As many possibilities as they generate, however, they almost always overlook another alternative—that of building a coalition. I think it is because, when we imagine the scene, we see in our mind's eye the master and the student. We all too often forget that there are others in the room, too. "Help me, friends!" you can cry to your fellow students. Although the master with the stick may be more powerful than the student, he is not more powerful than all the students put together.

A coalition can level the playing field. A good question to ask ourselves is "Who shares my interests or might be persuaded to work with me to make sure my needs are respected?" If you are faced with an abusive boss, it helps to gather support from other employees so that collectively you can confront the boss about his behavior. If an aging parent is refusing to give up driving a car when he is clearly a danger to himself and others, it helps to enlist your siblings' support. Rosa Parks and her colleagues used the power of a broad-based coalition of blacks and sympathetic whites to support her No to segregated busing. "There are two kinds of power in this world," community organizer Saul Alinsky liked to say, "organized money and organized people."

Ask yourself: "Who could be possible, if unlikely, allies in my situation?" If you are in sales, for example, it may be the end users for your products who could say a supportive word on your behalf to the purchasing representatives who are pressing you hard. If you are in politics, an unlikely ally may be a political opponent who nevertheless shares a common interest with you in promoting a particular piece of legislation.

One telling example of building a coalition as a Plan B is the story of a pilot in one of the first passenger planes to leave Denver shortly after the horrifying attacks of 9/11. Before the flight took off, the pilot announced to the fearful passengers: "If anybody stands up and is trying to take over the plane, stand up together, take whatever you have and throw it at their heads. You have to aim for their faces so they have to defend themselves." The pilot also encouraged passengers to throw blankets over the heads of any hijackers, wrestling them to the ground and holding them until he landed. "We the people will not be defeated," he declared.

"Everybody on the plane was applauding," said one passenger on the flight. "People had tears coming down their faces. It was as if we had a choice here, that if something were to happen we're not completely powerless."

That's the point. Remember that you are not alone.

Anticipate the Other's Power Moves

As you develop your Plan B, it is wise to think through the other's possible power moves. If you say No to the other's demand, what can they do to compel you to back down? And what can you do to empower your No so that you can continue to stand your ground?

Take Away Their Stick

If the other's reaction to our No is to hurt or threaten us, our first instinct may be to hurt them back. A more effective strategy, however, is to neutralize the impact of their behavior. If, as in the story of the Zen master, they are threatening to hit you with a stick, don't hit them back; just take away the stick. In other words, don't attack the other, but simply remove their ability to attack you.

Imagine that you are dealing with a difficult customer who makes an unreasonable demand on you to lower your price. If you say No, you anticipate based on previous history that his response will be to get angry and go over your head to your boss in order to get his way. One way to counter this tactic is to speak to your boss in advance and explain that the customer will likely come to ask her for a discount. Ask your boss to refer the customer politely back to you. If there is any potential for flexibility in pricing, it should be yours to show; otherwise the customer will always turn to the boss in the future, reducing you to the role of a messenger. When the customer then threatens to talk to your boss, you can say, "Please feel free. Here is her number." You have just taken away the customer's stick.

This strategy of taking away the other's stick without attacking them was used to great effect during the 1962 Cuban missile crisis. I had the privilege of participating in a meeting in Moscow in 1989 that convened many of the key participants who were still living. My colleagues and I listened spellbound as former U.S. secretary of defense Robert McNamara, former U.S. national security adviser McGeorge Bundy, former Soviet foreign minister Andrei Gromyko, former Soviet ambassador to the United States Anatoly Dobrynin, and others tried to piece together the full story of what really happened during those tense thirteen days in which the world's future hung in the balance.

Among the many lessons, one stood out for me. It was how close we came to Armageddon without intending it and how fortunate we all are that both U.S. and Soviet officials were so skillful with their Nos. As you may remember, the Americans had discovered that the Soviets had dispatched nuclear missiles by ship to Cuba, where they would target the United States. President Kennedy knew he had to say No but was unsure how to stop the Soviets without starting World War Three. He tasked a group of his closest political and military advisers to come up with a plan. The Plan B they devised in case diplomacy did not work was to order an air strike on Cuba and follow it with an invasion. For the first two days of discussion, they had no other plan. As we found out during those Moscow meetings, that Plan B, which came perilously close to being implemented, would in all likelihood have been disastrous. Unbeknownst to the U.S. leadership at the time, the Soviets had over forty thousand troops deployed, the Cubans had over two hundred and fifty thousand well-trained troops prepared to fight,

and, in case of American attack, the Soviet forces were autho-
rized to use nuclear missiles, some of which had already been
activated.

"That was horrifying," said Robert McNamara. "It meant
that had a U.S. invasion been carried out, if the missiles had not
been pulled out, there was a 99% probability that nuclear war
would have been initiated."

Fortunately, prodded by the president's brother Robert
Kennedy, the political and military advisers searched for a more
creative Plan B, one that, instead of attacking, focused on taking away the stick. The plan called for a quarantine of Cuba, a
naval blockade that would stop the Soviet ships carrying nuclear missiles from arriving in Cuba. That quarantine succeeded
in underscoring Kennedy's No and buying precious time for
Robert Kennedy and Anatoly Dobrynin to forge an informal
agreement whereby Soviet missiles were withdrawn from Cuba
and, as had been President Kennedy's intention all along,
American missiles were pulled out of Turkey. Without the constructive Plan B and the skillful diplomacy that followed it, we
might not be here today.

Consider the Worst Case

It can also be useful to think through in advance the worst-case
scenario. What is the worst thing the other can do to you if you
say No to them? The purpose of this exercise is not to create
unnecessary fear for yourself but rather to distinguish fear from
reality. As an executive once told me, "When I'm in a tough
spot in a business negotiation, I find it helpful to ask myself, 'What's the worst thing they could do to me? If they're
not going to literally *kill* me, then I'm probably going to survive. I'll be OK.' Then I start to relax and can negotiate more
effectively."

He has a point. In moments of tension, we tend to let our anxiety and fear magnify the potential consequences of saying No. When we take a clear-eyed look, we come to realize that those consequences are usually not as bad as our imaginations can lead us to believe. Then, prepared for whatever comes, we can boldly stand up for ourselves and our concerns.

Reassess Your Decision to Say No

Now that you have uncovered your Yes and developed a strong Plan B to empower your No, you are in a position to ask yourself the question: "*Should* I say No?" The presumption may be yes, but it is always wise during your preparation process to reassess your decision. After all, saying No may carry significant costs and risks for you—and for the other. Saying No often means entering into contention with the other, and you will want to choose your battles carefully. Here is a way to think through your decision.

Ask Yourself Three Questions

In deciding whether to say No, it is wise to ask yourself three questions: "Do I have the *interest* in saying No? Do I have the *power*? Do I have the *right*?"

Do I have the interest?

Will saying No protect or advance a key interest of yours, worth buying a possible struggle with the other, especially now that you understand *their* interests? Listen to your inner voice. If your intention is clear and strong, that is a good sign to go ahead.

Do I have the power?

Do you have the ability to sustain your No and to ride out the other's forceful reaction? Is your Plan B sound? If so, that is a sign to go ahead.

Do I have the right?

In some situations, we may ask ourselves whether we are even allowed to say No. "Do I have the *right* to say No? Am I allowed to say No in this situation?"

In some situations, asking ourselves this question may be valid. If we have made a promise or signed a contract, it may not be right to break it. But in too many situations of abuse, inappropriate behavior, or unreasonable demands, we accommodate because we feel unsure about whether we have the right to say No. Battered spouses, for instance, ask themselves whether they have the right to leave the marriage. They do.

In the final analysis, the answer is that we all have the right to say No. It is our fundamental birthright as a human being. The hallmark of a free person is their right to make decisions for themselves and to take the consequences.

It is not always easy to say No, particularly to people on whom we depend. In case of doubt, it helps to remind yourself, after doing the work of preparation, that you have a compelling *interest* to say No, the *power* to say No, and the *right* to say No. When your interests, power, and rights are aligned, very little can stop you.

Remember that your duty is not to say Yes to the other, whoever they may be, but simply to give them respect, which you can do *as* you say No. Respect is the subject of the next chapter.

Chapter Three

RESPECT YOUR WAY TO YES

"Never take a person's dignity: it is worth everything to them, and nothing to you."

—*Frank Barron*

Now that you have prepared *yourself* to say No, your next challenge is to prepare the *other* to say Yes to your No. How, in other words, can you make it easier for the other to accept your No and respect your needs? How can you open a channel of communication that makes it possible for the other to hear and understand your No as essentially positive?

The problem with most Nos is that they intentionally or unintentionally *reject* the other. The other often takes our No as a personal rejection. That may not be our intent, but the other may well hear an implied message in our No: "You and your interests don't count." It is only human to feel embarrassed, hurt, excluded, or even humiliated when being told No about something that matters. Hearing a No that is negative and rejecting, the other will likely close their ears to our message and may lash out destructively, causing our relationship to suffer.

When I was involved as a third party in the intense political battling between government and opposition forces in Venezuela, I was struck that the deepest anger in the leaders on each side was triggered not by the political issues of power and control, but by the *disrespect* they each felt from their adversaries. The country's president Hugo Chávez raged to me about how his enemies called him a *mono* (a monkey), demonstrating it by screwing up his face in a monkey-like grimace. Meanwhile, a leader of the opposition bitterly complained to me that when he tried to visit the central cathedral to pray, as he had done all his life, he was taunted and threatened on the street, all because President Chávez had branded him an "enemy of the people." The feelings of shame and humiliation provoked by these acts of personal disrespect were palpable—and they significantly increased the likelihood of escalation into violence.

Disrespect takes its toll in every domain, from work to family life. Listen to this account from a parent, Linda, who, in saying No to her daughter Emily, undermined her in a social setting. "Emily had a few friends over and I scolded her in front of them—saying she had to do her homework before socializing. Later, Emily said, 'How do you think it makes me feel when you yell at me in front of my friends?' Suddenly, I realized how embarrassing that must be. I know how I would feel if someone was criticizing me in front of a client. I also realized that I'd do a much better job motivating Emily to do her homework if I asked her with respect—and in private."

The secret to preparing the other to eventually say Yes is not to *reject* them, but to do the opposite: *respect* them. Let the respect diminish and offset the sting of rejection. By respect, I do *not* mean being accommodating. I simply mean giving positive attention to others, listening to them, and acknowledging them as fellow human beings. Treat the other with the same sense of dignity with which you would like to be treated.

Adopt a Positive Attitude of Respect

There is a real-life story I heard years ago that, for me, best captures the power of respect. Terry Dobson, a young American living in Japan studying aikido, a Japanese art of self-defense, was suddenly faced one day with the challenge of how to say No to someone's dangerous behavior:

The train clanked and rattled through the suburbs of Tokyo on a drowsy spring afternoon. Our car was comparatively empty—a few housewives with their kids in tow, some old folks going shopping. I gazed absently at the drab houses and dusty hedgerows.

At one station the doors opened, and suddenly the afternoon quiet was shattered by a man bellowing violent, incomprehensible curses. The man staggered into our car. He wore laborer's clothing, and he was big, drunk, and dirty. Screaming, he swung at a woman holding a baby. The blow sent her spinning into the laps of an elderly couple. It was a miracle that she was unharmed.

Terrified, the couple jumped up and scrambled toward the other end of the car. The laborer aimed a kick at the retreating back of the old woman but missed as she scuttled to safety. This so enraged the drunk that he grabbed the metal pole in the center of the car and tried to wrench it out of its stanchion. I could see that one of his hands was cut and bleeding. The train lurched ahead, the passengers frozen with fear. I stood up.

I was young then, some 20 years ago, and in pretty good shape. I'd been putting in a solid eight hours of aikido training nearly every day for the past three years. I like to throw and grapple. I thought I was tough. Trouble was, my martial skill was untested in actual combat. As students of aikido, we were not allowed to fight.

"Aikido," my teacher had said again and again, "is the art of reconciliation. Whoever has the mind to fight has broken his connection with the universe. If you try to dominate people, you are already defeated. We study how to resolve conflict, not how to start it."

I listened to his words. I tried hard. I even went so far as to cross the street to avoid the chimpira, the pinball punks who lounged around the train stations. My forbearance exalted me. I felt both tough and holy. In my heart, however, I wanted an absolutely legitimate opportunity whereby I might save the innocent by destroying the guilty.

This is it! I thought to myself, getting to my feet. *People are in danger and if I don't do something fast, they will probably get hurt.*

Seeing me stand up, the drunk recognized a chance to focus his rage. "Aha!" He roared. "A foreigner! You need a lesson in Japanese manners!"

I held on lightly to the commuter strap overhead and gave him a slow look of disgust and dismissal. I planned to take this turkey apart, but he had to make the first move. I wanted him mad, so I pursed my lips and blew him an insolent kiss.

"All right!" he hollered. "You're gonna get a lesson." He gathered himself for a rush at me.

A split second before he could move, someone shouted, "Hey!" It was earsplitting. I remember the strangely joyous, lilting quality of it—as though you and a friend had been searching diligently for something, and he suddenly stumbled upon it. "Hey!"

I wheeled to my left; the drunk spun to his right. We both stared down at a little old Japanese man. He must have been well into his seventies, this tiny gentleman, sitting there immaculate in his kimono. He took no notice of me, but beamed delightedly at the laborer, as though he had a most important, most welcome secret to share.

"C'mere," the old man said in an easy vernacular, beckoning to the drunk. "C'mere and talk with me." He waved his hand lightly.

The big man followed, as if on a string. He planted his feet belligerently in front of the old gentleman, and roared above the clacking wheels, "Why the hell should I talk to you?" The drunk now had his back to me. If his elbow moved so much as a millimeter, I'd drop him in his socks.

The old man continued to beam at the laborer.

"What'cha been drinkin'?" he asked, his eyes sparkling with interest. "I been drinkin' sake," the laborer bellowed back, "and it's none of your business!" Flecks of spittle spattered the old man.

"Ok, that's wonderful," the old man said, "absolutely wonderful! You see, I love sake too. Every night, me and my wife (she's 76, you know), we warm up a little bottle of sake and take it out into the garden, and we sit on an old wooden bench. We watch the sun go down, and we look to see how our persimmon tree is doing. My great-grandfather planted that tree, and we worry about whether it will recover from those ice storms we had last winter. Our tree had done better than I expected, though especially when you consider the poor quality of the soil. It's gratifying to watch when we take our sake and go out to enjoy the evening—even when it rains!" He looked up at the laborer, eyes twinkling.

As he struggled to follow the old man's conversation, the drunk's face began to soften. His fists slowly unclenched. "Yeah," he said. "I love persimmons too. . . ." His voice trailed off.

"Yes," said the old man, smiling, "and I'm sure you have a wonderful wife."

"No," replied the laborer. "My wife died." Very gently, swaying with the motion of the train, the big man began to sob. "I don't got no *wife*, I don't got no *home*, I don't got no *job*. I'm so *ashamed* of myself." Tears rolled down his cheeks; a spasm of despair rippled through his body.

Now it was my turn. Standing there in well-scrubbed youthful innocence, my make-this-world-safe-for-democracy righteousness, I suddenly felt dirtier than he was.

Then the train arrived at my stop. As the doors opened, I heard the old man cluck sympathetically. "My, my," he said, "this is a difficult predicament, indeed. Sit down here and tell me about it."

I turned my head for one last look. The laborer was sprawled on the seat, his head in the old man's lap. The old man was softly stroking the filthy, matted hair.

As the train pulled away, I sat down on a bench. What I had wanted to do with muscle had been accomplished with kind words. I had just seen aikido tried in combat, and the essence of it was love. I would have to practice the art with an entirely different spirit. It would be a long time before I could speak about the resolution of conflict.

This extraordinary story illustrates an everyday possibility: the surprising power of respect. The old gentleman used a few simple gestures of common respect—paying attention, listening, acknowledgment, and recognition—to disarm a dangerous individual and say No to violence. The same power of respect is available to us as well.

Respect is a positive attitude any of us can choose to adopt at any time. It starts with self-respect.

Begin with Self-Respect

Before we can truly give respect to the other, we need to give respect to ourselves because it allows our respect for the other to be genuine. Clearly, the elderly gentleman on the train respected himself, as shown by his easy confidence and his willingness to share scenes from his home life with a complete stranger—a potentially violent one at that. Self-respect creates the emotional and mental space that allows us to truly see the other. That is why the very first step of the Positive No method—uncovering your Yes—is essentially about self-respect.

You begin by paying positive attention to yourself—to your emotions, interests, and needs. You then move on to respect the other, which requires extending your circle of respect so that you see the other as a fellow human being who also has emotions, interests, and needs.

Respect, in the sense that I am using it here, is not something that needs to be earned by virtue of good behavior; every human being deserves it simply by virtue of being human. Even enemy warriors in extreme circumstances are able to show this kind of basic respect. During the Second World War, for example, British prime minister Winston Churchill signed a letter addressed to the Japanese ambassador which declared war on Japan with a typical Victorian flourish:

I have the honor to be, with high consideration, Sir, Your obedient servant, Winston S. Churchill

"Some people didn't like this ceremonious style," writes Churchill. "But after all, when you have to kill a man, it costs nothing to be polite."

As Churchill realized, showing respect comes not from weakness and insecurity but rather from strength and confidence. Respect for the other flows directly from respect for self. You give respect to the other not so much because of who *they* are but because of who *you* are. *Respect is an expression of yourself and your values.*

Take a Second Look

Respect does *not* mean liking the other personally—because you may not. It does *not* mean doing what the other wants—because you are about to do the opposite. What respect does mean is simply *to give value* to the other as a human being just as you would like others to give value to you. The old Japanese gentleman on the train gave value to the laborer.

The word *respect* comes from the Latin *re-*, meaning "again" (as in *rerun*) and *spectare,* meaning "to look" (as in *spectacles*). To respect, in other words, means to look again, or, as the dictionary puts it, "to notice with attention." That attention helps you to take a second look, to recognize the human being behind the aggravating behavior or objectionable demand.

When we respect the other, we are giving ourselves the opportunity to look again at someone whom fear and anger may have kept us from seeing fully. We are learning to observe people as they truly are, to listen for their underlying needs, to look for what is really going on inside them. To be respected means to be seen and to be heard—every human being deserves that chance.

We may not *feel* any respect toward the other at the moment. But even though we may not have much choice over what we feel, we do have a choice over how we act. Basic respect begins with concrete *behaviors,* such as listening and acknowledging, which may (or may not) lead to genuine feelings of respect. The important thing for the moment is to *act* with respect, whatever your feelings may be.

Respect Them for *Your* Sake

Giving respect to the other may sometimes seem like the last thing we feel like doing. "After what he did to me, no way! Why should I?" We may feel that person doesn't deserve our respect, particularly if he is acting disrespectfully toward us. Since these feelings are perfectly natural, it is important to understand why giving respect serves *our* interests.

"When I'm dealing with an armed criminal, my first rule of thumb is simply to be polite," explains Dominick Misino, who in his career with the New York Police Department negotiated more than two hundred hostage incidents, including a plane hijacking, without losing a single life. "This sounds trite, I know, but it is very important. A lot of times, the people I'm dealing with are extremely nasty. And the reason for this is that their anxiety level is so high: a guy armed and barricaded in a bank is in a fight-or-flight mode. To defuse the situation, I've got to try to understand what's going on in his head. The first step to getting there is to show him respect, which shows my sincerity and reliability."

Hostage negotiators such as Misino specialize in saying No. They cannot agree to the hostage taker's demands for freedom, so the challenge is how to say No and still get to Yes—the safe release of the hostages and the peaceful surrender of the hostage taker. The key first step is respect.

An obvious reason to give respect to the other is *because it works*. In my own work as a mediator in ethnic wars, I have had to deal with leaders who have blood on their hands. I do not approve of their behavior, I may not like them personally, but if I want them to accept a No to violence—bring about a cease-fire, save the lives of children—the only way I have found that works is to approach them through basic human respect.

The other is more likely to pay attention to us if we pay attention to them first; they are more likely to listen to us if we listen to them first. In short, they are more likely to respect us and our interests if we respect them and theirs.

"I have a real strict policy with my kids," says Celia Carrillo, a dedicated teacher in a school in a tough, low-income neighborhood. "It takes me about two to four weeks at the beginning of school to establish the policy. I just lay down the law that no one will call anyone names, and I just push respect, respect, respect. I believe that if I respect my kids, they will respect me and I have never found that to be any different. I'm not saying I get the best kids, but by the time they leave my classroom everybody wants to have my kids because they have learned respect and manners. For the most part, kids are starving for affection and for respect. They are so used to getting yelled at by their friends or at home, when they find you are not yelling back at them, they appreciate it and they learn to respect in turn."

Remember that in saying No, you are telling the other something they probably do not want to hear. Respect tends to make the other more receptive to understanding your message instead of simply dismissing it. It can diminish the intensity of a negative reaction and enhance the chances of a favorable response. *The more powerful the No you intend to deliver, the more respect you need to show.*

"If they listen to us, it is because we give them what they most want: respect," said one French Muslim community mediator who interceded to say No to the rioting by Muslim youth in France in November 2005. "If you respect them, they respect you.... We went right between the two sides and a lot of the kids listened to us. The damage the next day was a lot less serious than the previous nights."

In addition to establishing a short-term connection, respect can help build a longer-term relationship. A relationship of mutual respect greatly enhances your ability to influence the other. Giving respect is the equivalent of making a deposit in the bank of personal goodwill so that you can then make a withdrawal when you face a difficult situation.

Respect is the cheapest concession you can give the other. It costs you little and gets you a lot. It is probably no coincidence that the most successful car company in the world, Toyota, makes respect—for employees, business partners, host communities, and of course customers—one of its core guiding principles.

Respect, in short, is the key that opens the door to the other's mind and heart. When you give respect to the other, don't think of yourself as doing them a favor. Think of it as doing *yourself* a favor—because in the end it can help get *your* needs met. Respect makes sense not only because it is the right thing to do, but also because it is the *effective* thing to do. Respect the other for your *own* sake.

There are two principal ways to demonstrate your positive attitude of respect: listening and acknowledgment.

Listen Attentively

Perhaps the simplest way to show respect is to listen with positive attention. Listen to what the other is trying to communicate. Listen for what underlying interests and needs may be driving them. Recall the old saying that God gave us two ears and one mouth for a reason.

Many years ago, I was a guest on a talk show and a caller asked for advice about how to deal with her five-year-old son, who was exasperating her. "He never listens to me! What can I do?" I thought for a moment and asked the caller, "Well, do you listen to him?" There was a silence on the line before she replied: "No, but . . . "

Listening may be the last thing you feel like doing, especially if the other is behaving offensively. "Why should I listen to them? They should be listening to me!" you might think. But how can you expect them to listen to you if you do not listen to them? Indeed, when you are about to deliver an important No, listening may be the most effective way to prepare the other to hear and understand *your* message.

In one tough union-management negotiation headed straight for an impasse and destructive strike, the union representative decided to try a different approach before delivering his No to management's demands. Instead of countering management's story of financial woe, he simply started listening. He paid genuine attention to what they were saying. He asked lots of questions. His management counterparts were taken aback—this had never happened before. As they reported later, they felt heard and respected. That was the word they used—*respected*. In return, they began to develop more respect for the union representative. Thus when it came to the union's turn to explain their needs, management began to listen to the union. This surprising exercise in mutual listening proved to be the turning point in the negotiation. The devastating strike that was widely expected by all never materialized. Listening may be hard, but the rewards can be great.

So show your respect by letting the other have their say. Try not to interrupt. Indeed, do the opposite: when the other has finished talking, surprise them positively by asking them if they have anything more they want to say. It is remarkable how much useful information you can learn by listening and how much more effective your No can thereby become.

Listen to Understand, Not to Refute

All too often in tense situations, if we do listen, we listen simply to be able to refute what the other is saying. We treat the dialogue as if it were a debate and its key objective to score points. That may be appropriate for a debate, but it is not genuine listening. Here the key objective is not to hear or even to remember the other's words but to understand their underlying meaning.

" 'Talk to me'...is really our philosophy," explains police hostage negotiator Hugh McGowan. "It's not, 'Here I am, I'm on the phone and I want you to listen to me, here's what I am telling you to do, drop the gun, bop, bop, bop, you know.' That's not really what we're all about. It's '*You* tell me, Mr. Hostage Taker, Mr. Barricaded Individual. What's the problem? What's going on? What can we do to help you with your situation? You talk to me.' "

Just as police hostage negotiators begin their Nos by listening to the hostage taker, so you can begin your No by trying to understand the other. What is going on for them? By putting yourself in their shoes, you will be much better able to influence the other and persuade them to do what you would like them to do.

Just as you have probed behind your No for your underlying interests, needs, and values, now do the same for the other. Ask yourself what is the underlying interest behind their request or demand. What interests might be motivating their problematic behavior? Probe deeply. You may not always be able to satisfy these interests, but understanding them and taking them into consideration are essential if you are to persuade the other to accept your No and at the same time preserve the relationship.

You may fear that trying to put yourself in their shoes will only distort your judgment and weaken your resolve. But even if you consider the other to be your mortal enemy, remember that the first rule of warfare is to know your enemy.

When Nelson Mandela was in prison, one of the first subjects he undertook to study was Afrikaans, the language of his enemy. It was surprising, even shocking, to many of his comrades, but he studied the language intensively and asked his comrades to do the same. Mandela then proceeded to delve into the history of the Afrikaner people and the tragedy of the Boer War, acquiring a profound understanding of their group psychology and culture. In the process, he developed a deep respect for the Afrikaners—for their spirit of independence, their religious devotion, and their courage in battle. This understanding of the other side proved of enormous help later when it came to persuading the government to accept his forthright No to the cruel and unjust system of apartheid.

Ask Clarifying Questions

If you are not sure why the other is making a demand or engaging in inappropriate behavior, don't just guess, ask. Ask clarifying questions such as, "What's the problem here?" Or "Can you help me understand your needs?"

Consider the challenge of saying No to a key customer. This was the dilemma faced by software developers of a large well-known computer company whose clients were constantly demanding custom solutions based on a limited understanding of the software technology available. For a long time, the software developers said Yes, trying to provide good customer service, but the solutions proved too time-consuming and expensive, leaving the customer dissatisfied and the developers' bosses complaining about costs. Yet a straight-out No would also leave the client very unhappy.

Then the software team discovered the benefits of asking "Why?" and trying to uncover the customer's underlying need. They asked, "And *why* would that feature help you?" At first, the customers were a little reluctant to talk about their business needs with tech people, but when they discovered that there were usually features already available that could be configured for their purposes—drastically reducing lead time and cost— they eagerly responded to the new approach. That is the power of asking clarifying questions.

Sometimes, when you are about to say No to someone, there has been a misunderstanding and you are not in complete possession of the facts. One way to show respect is to give the other the benefit of the doubt—until you check out the facts yourself by asking clarifying questions.

Acknowledge the Other

Listening and asking questions are good first steps, but often you need to go further. In business and in politics, as at home, everything in the end is personal. If you do not acknowledge the other person first, regardless of your feelings about their behavior, you cannot expect them to hear your No, to understand it, and to accept it. If you want the other to accept your No rather than react punitively, you need to go out of your way to make sure your No is not heard as a personal rejection. This calls for a dual message: as you say No to the problematic request or behavior, say Yes to the person.

Acknowledgment does *not* mean agreeing with the other. It does *not* mean making any substantive concessions. It does *not* mean holding the other in high esteem. All it means is *recognition*. All human beings have a basic need to be recognized. Acknowledgment means treating the other not as a nobody but as a somebody, a fellow human being who exists and has needs and rights like anyone else. *Acknowledgment is perhaps the essence of respect.*

In a tense situation, it is natural and common to resist acknowledging the other. At a heated moment during a conference I once facilitated among leaders from the different sides in the Venezuelan conflict, the rector of the Catholic University in Caracas stepped in to make a powerful statement: "Let us start by getting three things straight," he announced. "First, the other exists. Second, the other's interests exist. Third, the other's power exists." His intervention was right on target—for the lack of basic acknowledgment of the other was a central obstacle to making progress in Venezuela. The monsignor's three acknowledgments are a good reminder for anyone involved in conflict, large or small.

Consider the approach taken by Bob Iger, Michael Eisner's successor as CEO of Disney Corporation, to quell a shareholders' revolt. Frustrated and angry at Eisner's policies and personal attacks, Walt Disney's nephew Roy Disney, together with investor Stanley Gold, had resigned from Disney's board and had run a Web-based campaign against Eisner that resulted in a shocking 45 percent of shareholders withholding their votes from him at the company's annual meeting. When Iger, who was Eisner's preferred candidate, was chosen as CEO, Roy Disney and Stanley Gold sued the company's directors, accusing them of rigging the selection process. So the first thing Iger did upon getting the top job was to pay a personal visit to Roy Disney and ask him to become a consultant to the company with the title of director emeritus. In other words, he acknowledged Roy Disney's concerns and affirmed the value of his many years of loyal service to the company. Roy Disney agreed to end the shareholders' revolt and take down the Web site. "All Mr. Iger had to do was show some respect to Mr. Disney," writes the *Economist* magazine. A little bit of respect can go a long way.

Acknowledge the Other's Point of View

One way of acknowledging the person is to acknowledge their point of view—without agreeing with it.

In response to the other's request, you might say, "I understand your problem. I've been there myself. *And* I cannot do what you are asking." Or you might thank someone for an invitation: "I appreciate your thinking of me. Regretfully, I am not free at that time."

In response to the other's inappropriate behavior, you might give them the benefit of the doubt. If the other is smoking in the office, it does not hurt to preface your request for them to stop with an acknowledgment that perhaps they did not know the office rules: "The No Smoking sign is a little hard to see. May I ask you please to smoke outside?" Even if they did see the sign, this approach helps them save face, giving them a second chance to choose an alternative behavior.

Starting from the other's perspective helps you connect with them so that you can then deliver your No. Faced with saying No to a youngster with a lit match, the boy's aunt exclaimed, "Ah! You've done it! It *does* light! Do you know how long it took humankind to discover the power of fire?" Then she explained firmly why he should not light any more matches: "Now that you know how, I want to ask you to promise me you won't do it again. It is dangerous and can burn down the house." Instead of reacting immediately with fear and anger, as she might easily have done, she connected with him and his delight, *then* she said No.

Let Them Know You Value Them

I once had a U.S. Marine base commander as a participant in one of my Harvard seminars. He had traveled all the way from his base in Japan because he wanted to improve his negotiating skills. At the end of the course, he came up to say that the one lesson that had struck him most was the importance of showing respect. It had suddenly occurred to him that the reason he was having so much trouble dealing with his teenage son was that he was not showing his son enough respect. He resolved to do a better job of letting his son know how much he valued him and respected his point of view even in the midst of their disagreements.

If saying No will create tension in your relationship, it is helpful to begin by affirming that relationship. A friend of mine was going through a trial separation with his spouse. Tensions were so high that it was difficult for the two to have a conversation about sensitive financial issues. What worked, he found, was to affirm their relationship before taking up the issue at hand, making clear that the relationship was larger than the issues dividing them. He also found it very helpful to do small things together such as jointly preparing a family meal with their daughter, which reminded them of what united them.

Affirming the other's value can have long-lasting consequences, bringing adversaries into a genuinely respectful relationship with each other. Listen to Danna Smith, who spearheaded an environmental boycott campaign targeting Staples, the office supplies retailing giant, for selling paper products made from cutting down old-growth forests: "We made a point during the campaign to build a constructive relationship with the executives. We tried very hard to make them understand that we were hard on the issues but that we valued the people that worked in the company and we knew that it was not their personal intent to destroy the forests."

While it was perhaps an unusual tack for environmental groups, who often see businesspeople as the enemy, it was precisely this kind of respectful approach, soft on the people while hard on the problem, that ultimately succeeded in persuading Staples to adopt environment-friendly practices. In the words of Joe Vassalluzzo, vice chair of Staples: "What was a terribly adversarial situation has much improved. I'm not saying we agree on everything, but I think there has been a greater meeting of the minds as a result of our communication process. The differences continue but it's in a much more collaborative and positive environment. Attitudes have changed for the better." That is what a little respect can do.

Surprise Them with Recognition

One of the greatest powers you have is the power to surprise the other with a gesture of recognition.

Listen to the story of Troy Chapman, a prisoner with whom I've corresponded, who is currently serving a long sentence in a federal prison. Chapman writes about how "a man was trying to walk me off the sidewalk. This is common in prison as scared and angry young men try to show how tough they are. Having dealt with similar situations for years, I'd always seen them in terms of two choices: back down or go on the offensive. This time another option suddenly occurred to me. I still remember the confusion in the man's eyes as I stepped off the sidewalk, touched his elbow, and said, 'How's it going?' *I stepped aside, but I didn't back off.* I engaged him, but on a different playing field. He was at a loss and simply mumbled some reply and kept walking. But I had told him in a language we both understood, 'I have no need of an enemy.' "

Instead of attacking or accommodating, Chapman surprised the other man by acknowledging him as a fellow human being: "How's it going?" In effect, Chapman changed the game from the "enemy game" to the "respect game." Respect is the higher ground between backing down and going on the offensive. Chapman said No to the offensive challenge by saying Yes to the person. That is the transformative power of acknowledgment.

One of the most dramatic and surprising acts of acknowledgment in international politics was Egyptian President Sadat's journey to Jerusalem in 1977. "What I want from this visit," Sadat told a newspaperman during the historic flight that took him to Jerusalem, "is that the wall created between us and Israel, the psychological wall [of distrust], be knocked down." No visit could have been more surprising to the Israelis, for up to that time, no Arab leader had ever publicly recognized the State of Israel or even acknowledged its existence.

In his speech to the Israeli parliament, Sadat spelled out his call for an end to the Israeli occupation of Arab lands, just as he had done in Cairo. But this time, he dramatically acknowledged the existence of his adversary: "Israel has become an accomplished fact recognized by the whole world and the superpowers. We welcome you to live among us in peace and security." He thereby created a climate of mutual respect in which peace talks could take place. The resulting outcome was a peace treaty and the complete withdrawal of Israeli troops and settlements from the Sinai Peninsula.

Any of us can use the power of surprising recognition in daily situations. If you are faced with a tough situation—at home, at work, or in the larger world—in which you are trying to connect with the other and they are refusing to hear you out, it is worth asking yourself, "What would be the equivalent of flying to Jerusalem?" In other words, what action would so startle the other that the door would suddenly open to hearing your No?

Begin Your Positive No on a Positive Note

The purpose of acknowledgment is to set a constructive tone for beginning your conversation with the other.

A Latin American business leader once told me about a challenging meeting he and other business executives had recently had with their country's president. The executives had arranged the meeting to discuss their concerns about the country's economic problems and to suggest that certain economic policies be changed. In other words, they were saying No to the status quo. As they launched into their agenda, the business leader noticed—from a balcony perspective—how the president was growing increasingly defensive as the executives raised their issues of concern and made their suggestions. Feeling personally attacked, he was in turn attacking each speaker.

So the business leader interrupted the meeting, saying, "I'm sorry, Mr. President, but we seem to have gotten off on the wrong foot here. What we are here to do is to thank you for all the remarkable progress in economic reforms you have made in your first term and to see how we, in the business community, can help you extend these reforms in your second term." The result, the business leader told me, was that the president visibly relaxed, the meeting went on for twice as long as scheduled, and in the end the president invited the executives to serve as advocates for the business community with his government.

When you are about to say No, it is all too easy to jump into the subject, just as the business executives did in their meeting with the country's president. You may assume that the other will understand that your intention is constructive, but they may receive your feedback, as the president did, as a personal rejection. It is often wise to begin on a positive note with an acknowledgment.

"You did a great job putting together that presentation. But the business case is not compelling enough for us to pursue this application," said a customer to one of my seminar participants who later cited it as an effective No, commenting, "*It made me feel appreciated.* It was direct and concise and the No was said without any expression of negative emotion."

One way to begin on a positive note is to ask the other politely for their time and attention: "I'd appreciate a word with you" or "May I have a moment of your attention, please?" A respectful approach will help prepare the other to hear you and will help make your No seem like a reasonable and acceptable response to their request or behavior.

Think of yourself as, in effect, *inviting* the other into a constructive discussion, almost as if you were inviting them to a friendly sporting match. As one manager used to say with a smile in a thick Scottish brogue, "Come talk with me. I'd like to pick a bone with you."

As part of your invitation, let the other know that there is a benefit for them too, not just for you. You might say to your problematic co-worker, "I'd like to discuss something that I think will enable us to work more effectively together." To your spouse, you might say, "I want to talk with you about something that will help us communicate better." In other words, spell out the positive future you desire for both of you.

Prepare, Prepare, Prepare

We have now reached the end of the preparation stage. You have uncovered your Yes. You have empowered your No. And by adopting an attitude of respect, you have prepared the other to say Yes.

No matter how skillful you are, there is no substitute for effective preparation and practice beforehand. Take it from the boxing champ Muhammad Ali, who liked to point out, "I run on the road long before I dance under the lights."

Now that you have prepared yourself to say No, it is time to actually deliver your Positive No. We now move on to the second stage of the process.

DELIVER

6. PROPOSE A YES

5. ASSERT YOUR NO

4. EXPRESS YOUR YES

Chapter Four

EXPRESS YOUR YES

"Be like a tree in pursuit of your cause.

Stand firm, grip hard, thrust upward.

Bend to the winds of heaven.

And learn tranquillity."

—*Memorial dedication to forester Richard St. Barbe Baker*

Delivering a Positive No is the crux of the process, requiring skill and tact. It begins with an affirmation (*Yes!*), proceeds to establish a limit (*No*), and ends with a proposal (*Yes?*).

Imagine, for instance, that you are declining an invitation to speak to a local community organization: "It is good to hear from you and good to hear of all the valuable work the center is doing. *For family reasons, I am not taking on any additional commitments at this time. Next year, if you are still interested, I'd be happy to consider it.* Thank you for thinking of me." After the initial note of acknowledgment and respect, you begin the Positive No by expressing a *Yes!* to your interests ("family"). You proceed to assert your *No* in a matter-of-fact way that does not reject ("I am not taking on any additional commitments at this time"). You follow up by proposing a *Yes?*, an alternative solution ("next year, if you are still interested"). You end, just as you began, on a note of respect ("Thank you for thinking of me").

The sequence is not rigid, of course, as we will see, but this is the basic three-step structure of the Positive No, preceded and followed by gestures of respect.

In these next three chapters, we will explore, in turn, each of the three parts of a Positive No, beginning now with the first part, expressing your Yes.

The Purpose of Yes

Why not just jump immediately to the No? The short answer is that you need to set up your No for success.

A man I know had a son attending the Air Force Academy. He was very proud of this and had high hopes for his son. In the middle of his education, however, his son called him up and told him, "I now realize I was wrong about who I want to be, and I want to leave the Academy. It won't prepare me for the life I want to lead." Even though it was shocking and disappointing news for the father, he cited it to me as the best No he had ever received. "Why?" I asked. "Because it was heartfelt and reflective," the father replied. The son's No came across effectively because it was rooted in a Yes to who he was and what he wanted out of life.

Contrast this with a No that a client of mine received from a bank. "A loan agreement to which we had verbally agreed fell through when the lead bank backed out. The banker telephoned us and said, 'I've called to tell you that we no longer have an agreement. I can't tell you why, but it is not you. It is something else.' He would not explain further. I felt utterly powerless." The lack of explanation made the No very hard to receive.

When I ask participants in my seminars for the worst Nos they have received, the most commonly cited is the one they received as teenagers from their father or mother: "No. Because I said so, that's why!" It is a purely power-based No that shows no concern for the other. The participants are adults, often executives high up in their organizations, yet they still remember these Nos with frustration and anger. "I have never forgiven that approach," wrote one manager, who was told she could not take a long-planned, self-paid trip to Europe after high school.

Your initial Yes has two basic purposes: it *affirms* your intention and it *explains* to the other why you are saying No.

Affirm Your Yes

Fear and guilt often stand in the way of your saying No. Affirming your Yes roots your No in the power of your positive intention, demonstrating how committed you are to addressing your concerns. Your Yes infuses your No with conviction and strength.

When Nelson Mandela was captured and put on trial for treason in South Africa in 1964, he insisted on making a public statement in court, going against the advice of his lawyers, who warned him that his statement might trigger a death sentence. He believed that the opportunity to affirm his intention publicly to the people of South Africa was worth risking his life. His concluding words summed up his Yes: "During my lifetime I have dedicated myself to this struggle of the African people. I have fought against white domination, and I have fought against black domination. I have cherished the ideal of a democratic and free society in which all persons live together in harmony and with equal opportunities. It is an ideal which I hope to live for and to achieve. But if need be, it is an ideal for which I am prepared to die."

Affirming your intention is a creative act. You are taking the first step in creating a new reality. Mandela understood this and was willing to lay down his life for this new reality of freedom for all. His instincts proved right. His eloquent *Yes!* to freedom continued to resonate in South Africa, indeed in the world, until the day freedom arrived.

The essence of a Positive No is to *assert without rejecting*—to assert your interests without rejecting the other as a person. You stand on *your* feet not on *their* toes. Your initial Yes is the key to achieving this delicate balance.

Explain Your No

Because the other can easily misinterpret your No and attribute false motives to you, your Yes is an opportunity for you to clarify your motives in saying No. It offers you a chance to show the other that you are not seeking to reject them personally, but simply trying to protect what is important to you.

Consider the case of a senior executive who traveled a great deal and ate most of his meals in restaurants. He had suffered for many years from a heart condition that made it absolutely necessary that he eat *no* butter or oil. Often, when explaining his special dietetic requirements to waiters, he would encounter resistance and failure to follow through. They did not really understand his No, thinking he was some kind of crank making their lives difficult. He felt tempted to go on the attack, but this wasn't good for his heart, either.

So he decided to clarify his motives with a visual explanation of why it was so important to him. Grabbing a pen and drawing on the napkin, he would say politely but firmly, "Look, here are the three arteries to my heart. One is 100 percent blocked, another is 85 percent blocked, and the third is 65 percent blocked. My doctors say if I have any butter or oil, I'll die. So may I ask you please to take this fish back and have it grilled without any fat?" The executive found that the server inevitably responded willingly to this clarification of his motive.

How do you, in a concrete fashion, deliver this initial Yes? There are three principal tools at your disposal: *the*-statements that set out the facts, *I*-statements that explain your interests and needs, and *we*-statements that invoke shared interests or standards. As you construct your Yes, select the one—or the combination—that best suits you and your situation.

Use *The*-Statements

How do you refer to behavior that is inappropriate, offensive, or abusive, or to demands that are unreasonable or unwanted? A natural human tendency is to point a finger at the person: "The product was delayed because *your* team took so long to get organized and because *you* made too many changes."

Such *you*-statements, however, naturally make the other feel defensive and reactive. A more neutral and effective way to get the same information across is to replace *you* with *the*: "The product got delayed as a result of *the* many changes that were made." *The*-statements avoid conflating the person and the behavior. *The*-statements are a simple Yes to the facts. No blame, no judgment, just the straight facts. Note: a *the*-statement does not necessarily mean that the sentence begins with "the"; it means it is fact-based.

Stick to the Facts

Since the other may have a very different perspective on the situation, the more objective you keep your description, the harder it is for the other to challenge it and the easier it is to accept it as a basis for conversation.

My friend Katherine had an experience in which she was trying to co-manage a small volunteer organization with her colleague Tom, yet he kept making decisions without first talking with her. This upset her so much that she confronted him one day: "Tom, *you*'re always rushing ahead and making decisions without checking with me. *You* are extremely disrespectful!" Tom reacted defensively, of course, and a fruitless argument with mutual accusations resulted.

In her second effort to engage Tom, Katherine took a different tack. She began the conversation with Tom by acknowledging his work and then focused on the problem at hand, sticking strictly to the facts: "Two weeks ago, an announcement was sent out to the group for a meeting that you and I had not discussed beforehand. Then last Friday, the calendar of events, which had been on the home page, was moved to a different page. I don't remember being consulted on that decision either." Faced with the straight facts, Tom was able to understand precisely what behaviors were troubling her.

The key is to describe the problematic behavior plainly and neutrally, without an edge. Keep it clean and simple.

If you are upset because the other broke a promise, your first impulse might be to say, "You broke your promise! You're not trustworthy!" If, however, you would like to see the behavior change, it is more effective not to attack the person outright but to focus hard on the problematic behavior. Remind the other of the promise that was made: "On Sunday night at dinner, I understood you to say that you would take the garbage out on Tuesday morning. Tonight, when I came back, I noticed that the garbage is still in the garage, and it stinks." Be clear and specific, sticking to the facts.

When No means bad news for the recipient, it can be hard to deliver. A fact-based approach can help the recipient accept the No. "Charlie, I'm sorry to tell you that we decided to hire Al for the position of school superintendent. Our decision was based on the fact that he has had more experience at the central office level. Your qualifications were exemplary and it was a difficult decision." Charlie told me later that even though he was disappointed, he felt it was a very effective No, commenting, "I respected the process. It was fair. They stuck to the facts and their decision was reasonable."

Sometimes blunt candor is called for. "Look, let's be honest here," says the boss to the employee who didn't get the promotion he expected. "There are some serious problems with your performance on the job." The employee may not like hearing this, but in the end he may learn something very useful and, in any case, it serves him better than the boss being evasive. Being honest and straight with people can work well if you accompany the candor with empathy and respect.

Be hard on the problem, not the person.

Watch Your Words

Few tasks are more difficult—or more important—than learning how to describe the other's behavior without judgment or condemnation.

When my daughter Gabriela was in kindergarten, the bulletin board spelled out specifically what not to do: no pushing, no kicking, no punching, no hitting, no biting, and so on. While most of us do not push, kick, punch, hit, or bite when we deliver our Nos, we often attack the other in more subtle ways, with words, tone, and body language. Retraining ourselves requires learning to recognize the destructive impact of our words and the indirect ways in which blame comes out:

"Shoulding" on the other.
A common form of blame is to use the words *should* or *shouldn't*, which usually come laced with judgment: "You *should* learn how to behave better!" or "You *shouldn't* do that." A more neutral phrasing would be: "This behavior creates a problem for

both of us." A very useful practice is to try speaking to the other without using the word *should*. It will increase the other's receptivity to your message.

Judgmental or subjective language.
When you are describing the other's behavior, it is very easy to make judgments. Consider again the words Katherine said at first: "Tom, you're always rushing ahead and making decisions without checking with me. You are extremely disrespectful!" "Rushing ahead" is subjective language with a judgment attached to it. She was accusing Tom of going too fast. "Going ahead" would have been a more neutral way of describing the same behavior. Similarly, "extremely disrespectful" is a judgment. Katherine was imputing malign intention to Tom where it may not have existed.

Often the judgment is obvious, as in: "That is an unreasonable demand." Or "Your behavior is atrocious." Or "Ridiculous!" Other times, however, the judgment is expressed more insidiously, but in a manner that is still quite explicitly negative and judgmental. In the midst of a discussion between two work partners about the common fees they would charge for their professional services, one says to the other, "I don't want to charge the lower fees you suggest. I just don't want that kind of scarcity mentality." A more neutral phrasing would be, "I believe our services deserve a higher fee."

While it may feel satisfying to judge the other, even surreptitiously through the nuance of a word, it rarely escapes the other's notice. It stirs up emotions of anger, defensiveness, and resentment and makes it all the harder for them to understand what the problem truly is. Judgment thus ends up muddying your message. It is more effective just to present the facts and let the other draw their own conclusions. Instead of telling your client, "Your demand is totally unreasonable," stick to the facts: "If we were to make the changes you have requested, it would delay delivery of the product to you by three months and raise the cost by $100,000."

You can either sit in judgment of the other or you can say No effectively, but you cannot do both.

Categorical statements.
"You are *never* satisfied with my food. *Nothing* I do is *ever* good enough for you!" one spouse announces angrily to the other.

"What are you talking about?" comes the reply. "You're *always* so sensitive. It seems like *everything* I do ends up with you getting upset about it!"

"There you go again, *always* putting me down!" shouts the first. And on it goes. Categorical statements may express your emotional state, but they do not communicate clearly the nature of the problem, nor do they help solve it.

Notice the language of *never, always, nothing,* and *everything.* These are not factual observations but hyperbole. From one or a few offenses is drawn a categorical conclusion that puts the other in a box from which they cannot escape. A correctable problem is thus inflated into an impossible challenge. Naturally, the other becomes defensive, rejects the categorical allegation as untrue, and in the process ignores the specific offense.

Consider instead what might have happened if the first spouse had simply described the facts: "Last night, I noticed that you gave the food I cooked for you to the dog. And tonight, I see you doing the same. My feelings are hurt." Such judgment-free language—delivered in a neutral rather than sarcastic tone—is likely to produce a very different response from the other, one that can advance the conversation.

In short, don't blame, don't shame. Speak your truth openly, but don't do it with cruelty. Reserve your attack for the problem, not the person. As the adage goes, "Say what you mean, mean what you say, but don't say it mean."

Use I-Statements

Another very useful tool for conveying your Yes is an *I*-statement. An *I*-statement is a description of your experience rather than of the other's shortcomings. Since *I*-statements refer to your feelings and needs, they are more difficult for the other to challenge.

An *I*-statement can be combined with a *the*-statement as follows:

- *Describe the facts:* "When situation X happens…"
- *Express your feelings:* "I feel Y…"
- *Describe your interests:* "Because I want or need Z."

For example, when Katherine came back to Tom a week later, she said: "I'm sorry I lost my temper last week. When an important decision is made without consulting me, I get really upset because it makes me feel left out. I want to be included and to participate in decisions." The combination of *I* and *the* not only clarified what behaviors had upset her, but made it easier for Tom to accept her complaint.

Note that putting an *I* in front of a judgment does not automatically make it an *I*-statement. "I think you're an idiot" is not an *I*-statement. Using the word "feel" doesn't necessarily help either, as in "I'm getting the feeling that you're a liar." Watch out for *you*-statements masquerading as *I*-statements.

An *I*-statement is not just a mechanical reframing of words. Your tone and attitude matter even more than the words themselves. If you are feeling angry, fearful, or guilty, it is easy for those feelings to leak out despite the best wording. That is why the internal preparation you do beforehand is essential, for it enables you to transform negative emotion into positive intention.

Express Your Feelings

The poet William Blake wrote with great insight: "I was angry with my friend: / I told my wrath, my wrath did end. / I was angry with my foe: / I told it not, my wrath did grow."

If, in describing the facts, you seek to be objective, now is the time to be subjective. Speak in the first person if it is culturally appropriate. Instead of saying, "You disappointed me" or even "The situation is disappointing," say, "I feel disappointed." This is your chance to express the truth that lies inside you.

In speaking your truth, there is no need to make the other wrong. You may feel yourself to be in the right. But for you to be right does not require proving that the other is wrong. Katherine does not need to prove to Tom that he was wrong to exclude her from decision making. An "I'm right, you're wrong" argument can go on forever and never get you anywhere. Even if the other is clearly wrong, it may not be productive to frame the discussion that way. What counts at this moment more than who is right and who is wrong is what you feel and need— and what they feel and need.

Take responsibility for your feelings. In bringing up her need for inclusion, Katherine acknowledged to Tom that feeling left out was a particularly sensitive point for her.

Describing or expressing your feelings in a controlled fashion is different from venting them impulsively as a way of discharging them. Psychologists have found that venting at the other can be a counterproductive method for cooling down. Far from decreasing one's level of anger, angry outbursts usually increase it and, in fact, prolong an angry mood. A more effective approach is to go to the balcony first for clarity and purpose, then approach the other and simply describe how you feel.

Naming the truth of what is going on for you can have a real impact on the other and on your situation. Listen to the experience of a trainer from Impact Bay Area, an organization that teaches women how to defend themselves from physical attack: "One of the most powerful pieces of saying No is that it breaks through the veneer that many attackers try to put on violent encounters. They want to pretend, for as long as possible, that what is going on is normal social interaction. Saying No cuts through that by naming the truth of what's happening. In fact, naming the truth (e.g., 'I feel uncomfortable because it's late and you're standing too close to me. Would you back up please?') often de-escalates the situation. It says you're ready to stand by your truth/version of the encounter, instead of letting them frame it their way (e.g., 'You wanted me to come over')."

You can express not only negative feelings but positive ones. "The customer was demanding a serious price reduction," one manager told me, "so I said, 'We feel very strongly that our brand and technology are worth paying for, and here's why.' It really helped the customer understand how passionate we are about our brand and helped them appreciate the value of it."

Describe Your Interests

Once you have described your feelings, you can then explain your interests—simply, clearly, and cleanly.

My son Chris came home one weekend from college and described two very different Nos he had received recently from two young women in whom he had shown a romantic interest. The first young woman sent a friend of hers to drop hints that she was not interested in a relationship. That may have been fine in a culture that communicates indirectly, but in his more direct culture, Chris experienced the No as very strange, as if the subject was so problematic it could not be openly discussed. He ended up feeling distanced from his woman friend.

The second young woman took an opposite approach. She came to see him and told him she wanted to talk. During the ensuing conversation, she explained her interests. She did not know many people and was feeling a need to expand her social universe, so she did not feel ready for a romantic relationship and preferred to remain good friends. In the end, Chris, while disappointed, felt closer to her as a friend.

The difference between the two Nos was the *I*-statement that the second woman used to explain her underlying interests. She both protected those interests and at the same time strengthened, rather than weakened, the relationship by offering a sincere and honest explanation.

Expressing your Yes can be transformative, particularly for those who are inclined to accommodate and avoid. I have a friend, Frances, who was diagnosed with breast cancer. She did not feel well treated by her surgeon, who made her wait two anxiety-ridden weeks for the results of a worrisome biopsy. At first she was inclined to accept this poor treatment, fearful of losing the doctor's care, but then she decided to speak up and take responsibility for herself. For Frances, this meant telling her surgeon her concerns. She told him the straight facts, described her experience, and ended up announcing to him, "I deserve high-quality care and I have lost confidence in yours." Frances did not attack but simply stood up for herself and affirmed her interests.

The aftermath? Saying Yes to her own needs gave Frances a feeling of relief, energy, and above all self-respect. And it freed her to pursue her Plan B, seeking another surgeon. She moved on to what she called a "dream team of physicians who are off the charts in their caring and competency." And, as for the first surgeon, his nurse told Frances later that she was very glad Frances had spoken up because her candor would make things better for the next patient.

At times you may feel hesitant or concerned about how the other will respond to your No, even prefaced by an explanatory Yes. In times of doubt, remind yourself that you are not responsible for the other's reaction. You are responsible for expressing your feelings and interests clearly. You are responsible for delivering a respectful *I*-statement, and then it is up to the other to choose how to respond.

Use W*e*-Statements

If you feel uncomfortable articulating your interest as yours alone, concerned that your No may appear one-sided or selfish or contrary to team spirit, you may want to expand the frame from *me* to *we*. Appeal to a shared interest or invoke a common principle or an accepted standard. In other words, use a *we*-statement.

Appeal to Shared Interests

Your interests are rarely yours alone. They also include the common interests of the larger community, whether that is your family, organization, or community. For example, you may not feel good about saying to a customer, "I can't customize the product for you because it would cut into profits." But you could frame your interest as being common to the larger customer base. "In order to maintain the low prices that all our customers have come to expect, I cannot offer customized versions. Would you be interested in exploring whether there is a solution to your particular problem using off-the-shelf components?"

Consider how one manager, a participant in one of my seminars, carefully explained to her superiors why she wouldn't accept the new job they offered her by invoking not only her own interest but the interests of others in the company: "I work for a major corporation where it is very career-limiting to say No to a new job offer. I had just taken on a new role, had bought a new house, moved.... Then on a Thursday, I got a call. They wanted me to fly halfway across the U.S. on Friday for an interview ... and then to start in a new role on Monday. It was a lateral move, in manufacturing, where I had already worked for twelve years. I said, 'I need to think about it overnight.' They said that was impossible, the tickets had been purchased for the following day. So I said, 'Give me an hour.' And they agreed.

"I thought that if I said No, I would be destroying my chances of ever being offered a new position. How could I say No in a way that was good for the company? I thought about it for an hour, and then called them back. First, I thanked them for considering me for the role. Then I said that I had already had an opportunity to work in manufacturing, and that my taking the role would block someone else's opportunity, which they would need in order to progress in this manufacturing-driven company. Finally, I concluded by saying, 'Therefore, I would like to leave this opportunity on the table for someone else to take advantage of.' That was five years ago. And since then, I have been offered numerous new job opportunities."

Invoke Shared Standards

Another way to make your *Yes!* persuasive to the other is to base it on shared standards or values such as equality, fairness, or quality.

Consider a business example studied by management researcher Jim Collins and his team. When George Cain became CEO of Abbott Labs, the company sat sleepily in the bottom quartile of the pharmaceutical industry. One of the main reasons for the mediocre performance, Cain realized, was nepotism: the practice of giving choice positions to members of the family regardless of their ability. "Cain didn't have an inspiring personality ... but he had something much more powerful: inspired standards," writes Collins.

Cain's No to nepotism began with a *we*-statement, a strong *Yes!* to excellence. Cain, a family member and son of a previous Abbott president, made clear to everyone, including his relatives, that they could continue in their jobs only if they had the capacity to become the best executive in the industry within their span of responsibility. "Holiday gatherings were probably tense for a few years in the Cain clan. ('Sorry I had to fire you. Want another slice of turkey?')" notes Collins. But in the end, family members were happy with the financial results for, with his Yes to excellence and No to nepotism, Cain turned Abbott Labs into a top performing and highly profitable company.

An invocation of shared standards helped defuse an international incident during the 1962 Cuban missile crisis that could have triggered a world war. This story emerged from the same series of meetings described in an earlier chapter. Among the many close calls, perhaps the least known was what occurred aboard a Soviet submarine armed with nuclear torpedoes and submerged in the north Atlantic. A U.S. warship dropped depth charges on the sub, trying to force it to the surface where it could be tracked. To the Russian captain, with temperatures soaring and his boat running out of oxygen, this was an attack that called for retaliation. He ordered that the nuclear torpedoes be prepared for firing.

Russian naval procedure—the shared standard of behavior—required two other officers to agree to the firing. One second captain instantly agreed: "We're going to blast them now!" he screamed. "We will die, but we will sink them all! We will not disgrace our navy!" But the other second captain, Vasili Arkhipov, said No, reminding the other two that the naval regulations permitted firing only if the sub's hull had been breached, which it had not. "Arkhipov was a man who never lost his cool," explained a close friend of his years later. "The captain had lost his temper. The situation was very tense and everyone was swearing. Then, thank God, everyone calmed down."

"If that torpedo had been fired, nuclear war could have started right there," said Robert McNamara, commenting on the incident over thirty years later. One ordinary man, saying No at the right time and in the right way, may have saved the world.

Express Your Yes Without Saying "Yes"

If your No has nothing to do with reasons but simply with a gut feeling, there is no need to invent reasons or excuses. Imagine, for instance, that you are feeling uneasy about loaning a friend a significant sum of money. Your mind races through possible excuses for not doing so: "I may need the money myself." "My spouse would be upset if she found out." "I don't want to have to remind you if you forget to pay me back." None of these reasons really gets to the truth of the matter, which is simply that you don't feel comfortable loaning the money. This is a time to trust your intuition, which is an entirely legitimate reason for saying No, even if it is your only reason. So consider simply saying, "I'm sorry. I just don't feel comfortable doing it." Or "I'm sorry. I can't do it." And leave it at that.

If someone is asking you to do something you do not want to do, sometimes the best answer is the most direct: "I do not enjoy that kind of work." Enough said. There is no need for long speeches or excuses that only make your No lose force, no need to buy time with "ahs" or "ums." Keep your explanation short and to the point. Often, the shorter it is, the stronger it is.

While an explanation of your interests is usually the respectful thing to do, sometimes the most effective explanation is none at all. There is a saying in some Al-Anon circles that goes, "No is a complete sentence." What is meant is that, in certain circumstances, you don't need to explain your No to the other.

If you are refusing an alcoholic drink, for instance, you don't need to justify your refusal. A simple respectful "No thanks" will do. You know your Yes—that is essential—but sometimes you keep it to yourself, because it is your business and not theirs.

The photographer Philippe Halsman was famous for asking his subjects to allow him to photograph them in midair as they jumped. Richard Nixon, J. Robert Oppenheimer, Grace Kelly, and the Duke and Duchess of Windsor, along with many other notables, all agreed to being photographed in this pose. One day, as Halsman was concluding a shoot of pianist Van Cliburn, he asked if the pianist would jump for him—and Van Cliburn refused. In Halsman's words, "Politely I inquired what his reasons were for not wanting to jump. The artist put his arms behind his back, lifted his chin and said, *'There is no need for explanations.'*"

Halsman was so impressed by this matter-of-fact affirmative reply that he instantly took a photograph of Van Cliburn in this pose and included it prominently in his book of photos of famous people jumping, under the title "Van Cliburn Won't Jump." Halsman understood that Van Cliburn was saying Yes to his own unique preferences and his need for privacy, which is why Halsman was delighted rather than offended even though the message was delivered without explanation.

Yes! Is a Value Statement

When you express your Yes—and it truly comes from a deep and principled place inside you—it can change the way the other receives your No. Long ago, Bob Woolf, one of the preeminent sports agents of his time, told me a story that captures this truth.

When Larry Bird, the basketball superstar, was just about to begin his meteoric professional career, Bob Woolf got a call from a committee of prominent townspeople from Bird's hometown of Terre Haute, Indiana, to ask if Bob would be interested in being considered for the job of representing Larry Bird. Bob Woolf said yes, of course, and flew to the town for an eight-hour exhaustive interview with the committee which included the local university athletic director, the local bank president, the owner of the local department store, and other town elders. They wanted to know everything. After months of considering hundreds of applicants, the committee whittled down the list to twenty-five, then fifteen, and finally to three. Bob had his final interview in Terre Haute, and it went so well that he excitedly called his wife back in Boston to tell her that he was almost certain he would get the job.

As soon as he hung up the phone, a call came in from the committee who asked if they could come over. Ten of them squeezed into his hotel room and told him, "We have got to know from you what exactly you are going to charge as your fee for representing Larry.... Give us a dollar figure. We have got to know exactly what it is. Mr. Katz [the other candidate] has given us a figure and we need one from you."

Bob felt his stomach tighten. He had always worked on a percentage basis, not a flat rate. That was the working relationship with all his other clients and it had worked out fairly for all.

"Look," Bob replied, "I understand why you're asking me and I respect Larry's desire to know how much it will cost him. But I want to work with Larry the same way I have worked with everyone else. At the end of the negotiations when Larry has a contract, then we will agree upon a fee. I cannot give you a figure now. It wouldn't be fair to my other clients if I was to make a special adjustment in order to work with Larry. I want to represent him very much. I consider this a special opportunity. But I just can't give you the answer you want."

In other words, Bob explained the Yes behind his No.

The committee chair stared back at Bob. "Well, look, we just want to be sure that you understand the consequences," he said. "We're asking you again, give us a set figure and we can wrap this up. Chances are, I've got to tell you, that without it you will not be representing Larry Bird. Please give us a figure."

Bob took a deep breath. "I can't give you a figure. I can only repeat that my fee will be reasonable and I will work hard on Larry's behalf. But I will not treat Larry Bird any differently than anyone else I represent and I am prepared to accept the consequences."

They all shook hands and the committee members walked out of the room.

"You can only stand and look at a door for so long," Bob recalled. "I felt righteous but miserable." He called home again and told his wife, "You won't believe what just happened." His son got on the line and tried to console him. "It's all right, Dad, I'm proud of you. You still have your principles and I'm glad that's what you did."

Five minutes later, the phone rang.

"Bob, this is Lu Meis. I just wanted to tell you we've made our decision. We thought we shouldn't wait until morning to let you know."

"Yes?" Bob braced himself for the bad news.

"We've decided on you."

Bob couldn't believe his ears. "You're kidding!"

"No, Bob," Meis said. "We know how much you want to represent Larry, how much it means to you and how much time and effort you put into coming here. We decided that if you would stand up to us the way you did, stick to a position and just walk away, you are the kind of man we want negotiating for Larry with Red Auerbach."

In other words, they wanted an agent who could say No on behalf of a deeper Yes.

To sum up, the way to begin your No is with a Yes. Your Yes may take the form of a *the*-statement, *I*-statement, or *we*-statement, or a combination. You do not blame or shame the other. You don't reject the other. You simply assert your own interests, needs, and values.

Your Yes is essentially a value statement. You are asserting your value. It could be your value as a human being; in a commercial context, it might be the value of your product or service or brand; in a larger context, it could be your ethical and moral values. Ultimately, you are saying Yes to what truly matters.

After your Yes comes your No. That is the subject of the next chapter.

Chapter Five

ASSERT YOUR NO

> "It's easy to say 'no!' when a deeper 'yes!' is burning inside."
>
> —*Stephen R. Covey*

Now that you have expressed your Yes, it is time to assert your No. In our journey, we have come to the very heart of the Positive No method. We are not only in the middle of the three stages but also in the middle part of the Positive No statement. All else is prelude or postlude.

The essential action in asserting your No is very simple. You are setting a clear limit, drawing a clean line, creating a firm boundary.

The Power of No

Saying No is essential to life. Every living cell has a membrane that allows certain needed nutrients to pass through and repels others. Every living organism needs such boundaries to protect itself. To survive and thrive, every human being and every organization need to be able to say No to anything that threatens their safety, dignity, and integrity.

No is the key word of order, structure, and discipline. Rules and laws are often stated in the form of Nos. Of the Ten Commandments in the Bible, for instance, eight are framed as Nos. The great virtues of No are clarity and specificity. Just think of the difference between telling a child, "Please treat your classmates with respect" and saying, "No hitting!" "No" gets the point across simply and clearly, specifying with precision exactly what you mean.

There comes a moment in life when each person learns the power of saying No to set a protective limit. I once saw a little boy crying in my daughter's preschool playground. His schoolmates were swinging him on a tire hanging from a tree. He wanted to get off, but he could not communicate his feelings. As I watched, his teacher intervened. She gently instructed him to "use your words." He immediately started saying, "Stop the swing! Stop the swing!" When his schoolmates did stop, his face lit up with delight at his discovery of the power to say No.

But No has uses that go far beyond protection and discipline. When we make fun of children saying No, calling the age when they first learn to use that word the "terrible twos," we are missing the importance of the developmental work they are doing. For this is when children are becoming autonomous and learning to create boundaries. They are beginning to define who they are—and who they are *not*. If you listen carefully behind their Nos—"No, I don't want to eat that! No, I don't want to wear that! No, I don't want to go there!"—what do you hear? "I exist! I have a right to my own feelings. I have a right to my own opinions. I am me." A new being is announcing her independent existence. Learning to say No is essential to the ongoing development of each human being.

No is the key word in defining your identity, your individuality, or, in organizational terms, your brand. If you cannot say No, you do not have a brand, for your brand is defined by what you say No to. No is a selection principle that allows you to be who you are and not someone or something else. No gives you the individuality and definition that make this world a richer place.

Because No is the word we use to express our power, the normal tendency is to overdo our Nos, so they come across as attacking—or to underdo our Nos, so they come across as weak and hesitant. The challenge is to get it just right. How can you be assertive without being aggressive?

Let Your No Flow

The solution is to use what might be called a natural No.

A natural No is simple and straightforward. It flows naturally and almost effortlessly from your Yes. I remember hearing natural Nos from my daughter Gabriela when she was small. "No" would just roll off her tongue as if it were the most natural thing in the world. "No, I don't want to talk right now, Papi. I'm playing. Can I go now?" I would be five thousand miles away in a jungle, having tramped miles to find a phone to talk with her and having tried the line a half dozen times, but I always found myself utterly disarmed because her No was so natural. It was transparent, untamed by fear, unspoiled by anger. It was honest, clean, and matter-of-fact.

Nos get more difficult to say as we get older and our emotions and motivations become more complex and our sense of consequences more acute. But if you've followed the process this far, the action is, in one sense, already over. You've done the essential preparatory work. You are like an athlete who has trained hard. Now, during the race, it is time to reap the rewards of that hard work.

Let your No flow. Let it flow from the Yes you have uncovered. Let it flow from the power you have developed. Let it flow from the respect you have offered. In this way, your No will be clear, committed, and clean.

Let It Flow from Your Yes

Perhaps the most important thing to keep in mind as you say No is your Yes—the core interest, need, or value you are seeking to protect. Remember that *No is just a different way of saying Yes.*

Consider how this mother stands up for her child who has special needs when a teacher wants the child to leave the class:

TEACHER: I'm sorry, Mrs. Taylor, but Courtney can't stay in the humanities class. She doesn't belong there.

MOTHER (*in a matter-of-fact tone*): No. Courtney has a right to be included with her peers. We will have to find a way to make it work.

TEACHER: But she's not keeping up.

MOTHER: Courtney has challenges, but I assure you that she will do the work.

TEACHER: But she got upset the other day by the work.

MOTHER (*quiet and firm*): The reason she got upset was because she was told that she doesn't belong in the class.

Courtney stayed in the class and did the work.

The mother's No flowed naturally from her Yes—her desire to have her child feel included. The mother did not attack the teacher, saying things like, "You are discriminating against my daughter! You told her she didn't belong in the class." Instead she stayed focused on protecting Courtney's right to be included with her peers in the classroom. The mother was not laying down the law or driving a stake in the ground, but standing up strongly for her child.

As this example illustrates, a natural No is not a rigid and inflexible position, but rather a firm stance that flows organically from your interests. Remember, you are simply using the clarity, specificity, and power of a No to communicate a Yes to what matters.

Imagine your No not as a *wall* but rather as a strong living *boundary* that protects what is important. Whereas a wall creates a visual barrier between the parties, a boundary allows the parties to see each other and stay connected—while still setting firm limits.

Let It Flow from Your Power

Linguistic philosophers distinguish between messages that describe a situation and those relatively few messages that actually change the situation. They call the latter "performative speech acts." The classic example is when two people standing in front of a minister or judge say "I do." "I do" is not just a *description* of how they are feeling. It is an *action*. It transforms their social status from single to married.

Similarly, when you deliver a Positive No, you are not just describing your feelings or interests. You are conveying your commitment to a future course of action. You are not just saying No. You are ready to back it up with your personal power. Your intention is strong, and you are prepared to deploy Plan B if necessary. With your commitment you are creating a new boundary that did not exist before. You are changing social reality.

My friend David is a Native American who practices his ancestral religious tradition by building sweat lodges in the wilderness, sauna-like structures in which people pray as they feel the heat. One dry summer, the local authorities prohibited all fires, worried about the possibility of forest fires. David is extremely careful with fire. He never leaves a fire alone, always making sure a keeper of the flame oversees it day and night. When the fire marshal insisted that David stop practicing his fire ceremonies, David did not get angry. He simply lowered his tone of voice and uttered a deep, resonant, lingering No that came from his *Yes!* to his religious beliefs. "Noooh. We will continue to practice our religion as we always have, long before the Europeans came. It is our sacred custom to watch our fires all through the night. We have never caused a forest fire and never will. You are welcome to observe our precautions if you like." After that, no one interfered in David's religious practices.

That is it. The No is quiet, deep, and firm. The sound can sometimes extend almost as if you are physically laying down a line. You are not proposing a line or talking about a line, but actually drawing it with the power that comes from your commitment. You are creating a new reality.

Consider a business situation in which a No needs to be said to a key customer: "With one client, we had been negotiating for about six months. Finally, we put together what was really our last offer. We took three to four weeks to prepare it, taking into account the customer's needs. We used our top executive to deliver it. After he said, 'Here's what we've put together as our final offer,' the client responded by continuing to negotiate and ask for more. Our executive responded in a very calm, matter-of-fact tone, 'Perhaps you didn't hear me. This is our *last* offer.' In about five seconds, there was a complete flip in the conversation. The client said, 'Let me get my business guy on the phone to discuss the terms.' Now they valued us and what we could do for them."

The executive drew a line. He was not bluffing. He was conveying his commitment, signaling that beyond this point, he was prepared to resort to his Plan B, which was to walk away from this particular deal and pursue other clients. Your Plan B does not need to be stated, but it is nevertheless implied, underscoring the limit you are setting. Paradoxically, saying No can sometimes be a gift to the other. Once a clear line is drawn, the other can relax, strange as it may seem. The customer, in this case, felt more satisfied because he knew he had gotten as good a deal as he possibly could.

For conveying commitment, it helps to use a matter-of-fact tone, just as my friend David and the executive did. You are not attacking but simply announcing a new fact, which is the clear limit you are setting in response to the other's demand or behavior.

To get your No heard, there is no need to shout. There is no need to be aggressive, nor is there a need to placate. A firm, neutral tone will do just fine. Paradoxically, a No delivered in a low tone of voice can signal more determination than one delivered at high decibels.

You can be polite and firm at the same time. My friend Stephen describes how he once overheard his wife, Sandra, talking on the phone, responding to one of many requests to serve on a committee for a local fund-raiser. It is understandable in such situations to feel at a loss for words, to start stammering an excuse or two, explaining that you are overloaded. If pressed by the caller, it is all too easy to simply give in with a sigh of resignation. To Stephen's admiration, he heard Sandra reply in a calm, neutral tone, "I won't be serving on the committee this year. Thank you for thinking of me." That was it—polite, firm, and final.

Keep your tone matter-of-fact and neutral, and let your No flow naturally from your power.

Let It Flow from Your Respect

With a negative No, you distance yourself from the other. With a Positive No, you do the opposite. You move closer. You seek to stay connected with the other through respect.

When one successful Spanish bank has to inform an important client that they cannot fund a proposed investment, the matter is not left to a loan officer. The No is considered so important that it is delivered directly by one of the bank's owners. The owner doesn't just send a letter or make a phone call, trying to stay distant because it is uncomfortable to say No to an important customer. In fact, he does the exact opposite, seeking to bring the customer even closer. He invites the client out for a long lunch at the family hacienda an hour outside of Madrid. They enjoy a fine meal and a good talk. Afterward, as the banker and his client are sipping their liqueurs and smoking their cigars, the banker tells the client, "As you know, we value our relationship with you very much. We are very sorry that we cannot be of more help to you on this particular deal, not this time. We look forward to working with you on many other deals." The banker says No matter-of-factly with elaborate courtesy, making it clear how much he values his customer. The important message is delivered and the relationship is preserved. Saying No to a deal is such a special occasion that it is treated with the same care and ceremony that would be used to celebrate the successful conclusion of a deal.

"There are moments when people have to say No," says Luiz Inácio Lula da Silva, a trade union leader who started his life in extreme poverty and rose to become the president of Brazil, "and that No needs to be said with the same sincerity, the same honesty, and in the same tone of voice that people say Yes."

When you say No, you seek to stay connected, like the Spanish banker, in order to prepare the way for a positive result and relationship.

It is not always easy to say No nicely. We often make our Nos carry a lot of emotional baggage for us—our anger, fear, guilt, or shame. All that baggage just gets in the way of clear, effective communication. Try to keep your No as free of baggage as possible. That is why you have done the essential preparatory work of turning negative emotion into positive intention and developing an attitude of respect. It keeps your No clean.

Don't be overly concerned with what the other will think. Sometimes we see our task as "I need to tell them No in such a way that they aren't upset and they still like me." But this is an almost impossible task, because if you are trying to manage their reaction, you may end up losing sight of your own interests and values and, what is more, you are trying to control something over which you actually have no control. So instead, see your task as "I need to tell them No in a way that is clear, honest, and respectful, and then let them react however they react."

One of the great arts in life is learning how to disagree without being disagreeable.

Saying No to Demands

Below are some specific key words or phrases you can use in saying No to the other's demand in a way that flows naturally from your Yes, your power, and your respect. Remember that your tone and underlying intent need to be congruent with your words if they are to have the right impact.

"No" or "No Thanks"

The simplest word for setting a limit is *No*. It is a word of pure power. For those of us who shy away from the use of power and have a tendency to accommodate or avoid, it can sometimes be useful to begin our sentences with the word *No* in order to bring power back into our Nos. "No. I want you to eat food that is good for you, so you cannot fill up on ice cream before dinner," announces the parent to the child. The No has clarity and directness.

Directness has its place, but it can be expressed gracefully. In a newsreel of Mahatma Gandhi landing in England for peace talks with the British, we see eager reporters asking him to speak into the microphone, and he replies simply, "I think not," as he continues to walk away, smiling.

Adding a *thanks* to the No shows respect and care for the relationship. The *No* protects and the *thanks* connects. A simple, energetic, appreciative "No thanks" is often enough. If you are dealing with telemarketers who ignore your early response, you can say: "I'm saying No now. [Pause] Thank you! Goodbye."

"I Have a Policy"

One powerful way to frame the limit you set is in the form of a broader policy of which your No is but one instance. For example, "I have a policy of never serving on boards." Or "I make it a personal policy never to lend money to friends." Or "I never respond to phone solicitations."

When you say that you have a policy, you are signaling that your No is not a one-time message but an ongoing practice to which you have given a lot of thought. It is a signal of resolve, a sign that you will not budge. Of course, this phrase is not to be used lightly or misleadingly as a rigid adversarial position; it works when it is indeed your policy, something you have thought through.

Framing the limit you set as a policy also has the benefit of letting the other know that your No is nothing personal; it is independent of them and their behavior. It is essentially positive. You are not saying No to them as much as you are simply continuing to say Yes to the principles and values by which you have chosen to abide. In short, saying "I have a policy" affirms your interests, backs it up with your power, and gets your relationship off the hook by depersonalizing your No.

Consider the example of a textile manufacturer that was being constantly pressed by its customers for timely fulfillment of their orders. For years, the company responded by accommodation. When a customer would become angry at a delay, the manufacturer would typically respond by an "escalation"—rushing the order through and putting all other orders on hold. The outcome was a dysfunctional system and general dissatisfaction all around. Finally, the company's leaders faced the problem and hired a team of consultants to figure out a better system of just-in-time manufacturing. To make it work, they formulated a new policy for customers: no escalations. They announced the new policy and, despite the initial pushback from customers, stuck to it.

The end result? The policy of no escalations enabled manufacturing to greatly reduce the complexity of managing the factory and thus allowed the company to turn around orders within two weeks instead of the usual six. Now there were very few delays in orders and no need for escalations—a win for all sides.

"I Have Plans" or "I Have Another Commitment"

One concrete everyday phrase that can affirm your interests as well as your power without spoiling your relationship is "I have plans" or "I have another commitment at that time." In other words, let the other know that you have already accepted other responsibilities.

To the friend who is inviting you to a party, you can say, "I'm sorry. I have plans that night. Thank you!" To the co-worker who is asking you to take on a last-minute project, you can say, "I'd like to help you out, but I have other projects I am committed to finishing before I take on anything else." To the boss who is asking you to work this weekend on a project, you can say, "I'm sorry. I have an important family commitment this weekend." To the person who is asking you to take on a new civic responsibility, you can say, "I need to focus on my family/personal life/work/studies right now."

One client of mine was proposing a very good deal to a new customer. The reply: "Since we have an agreement with your competitor, I cannot consider your offer at this time." My client felt this was one of the more effective Nos he had ever received because "it claimed the moral high ground by demonstrating that they keep their deals." They let him know that if he did business with them in the future, he could expect the same kind of honesty and commitment that they were showing toward his competitor.

"Not Now"

It is not easy to say No, especially if you have an important relationship with the other. One way to soften the blow of the No for them, and thus make it easier for you to say No in these circumstances, is to locate your No in time. In other words, use the magic phrase "Not now."

A customer who is asking you to develop a special technological solution to their problem will find it easier to hear "I'm sorry, but we are not able to provide this kind of solution right now" than to hear a blanket No. Similarly, an employee who is asking you for a raise will find it easier to hear "I'm sorry, but given current economic conditions, it is not possible at the present time." One employee I know who received this response felt it was effective because "I felt heard, and it left the door open to a Yes in the future."

To be sure, "Not now" does leave the door open to a future request. So if you are certain that it will *never* be possible for the employee to have a raise, the customer to have their technological solution, or your child to have a motorcycle, it is usually better to let them know that now. "Not now" is intended for those cases where there does exist a real possibility for addressing the other's needs in the future.

If the other presses you with "If not now, when?" and you do not know, you can say, "I can't say. We'll have to see," or "I'm sorry, but I can't tell what the future will bring."

If the other persists in pressing you hard for an immediate answer to their request and you do not wish to be rushed into a premature decision, you can always respond by saying, "If you need an answer right now, the answer is No." The other may suddenly discover that they *do* have the time after all to wait for your considered decision.

"Not now" is a very useful phrase, particularly if you are in doubt. It is better to say "not now" and change your answer later to Yes than it is to say Yes and try to change your answer later to No.

"I Prefer to Decline Rather Than Do a Poor Job"

A school headmaster I know uses this rule of thumb when being asked to take on new responsibilities: "Can I do a good job?" he asks himself. "Do I have the time to do the matter justice, and do I have the skills?" If the answer is No, he says an outright No to the other. His No is actually a Yes to effectiveness and quality standards.

When you decline rather than do a poor job, you are not only affirming your own interests but also paying attention to the relationship. You will *both* be worse off—and so will your relationship—if you say Yes and then do a job that turns out to be unsatisfactory.

An electronics company, a client of mine, was asked by a leading customer for a new custom-designed product with a tight delivery date. The company's sales vice president was very tempted to say Yes, but he and his colleagues realized that their production was already under strain and the chances of meeting the customer's deadline at quality standards were not good. So they said No to the customer, thereby sparing themselves and their customer a lot of dissatisfaction. "It was very hard to do at the time, but it was the best No I ever delivered. And the customer came to appreciate it too, and valued our honesty with them up front," reflected the sales vice president to me later.

Sometimes the other is asking you to do something simply because they feel insecure about their own abilities. In this case, you can follow up and tell the other, "*You* will do a much better job! I have confidence in you." Give them encouragement as you say No.

In short, know your limits, acknowledge them freely, and spend your time on what you can do well. Both you and the other will be better off in the long run.

Saying No to Behaviors

In international diplomacy, a key term is *demandeur*, French for "asker." In any transaction, the question is, "Who is doing the asking?" When you say No to the other's requests or demands, *they* are in the role of asker. But when you say No to the other's behavior, *you* are in the role of asker. A Positive No takes a slightly different form when *you* are asking *them* for something.

Here are some useful phrases for saying No to an inappropriate behavior.

"Stop/No!"

When you are setting a limit to behavior, the words of power are *stop* and *No*. In a case of sexual harassment, for example, *stop* is the operative word: "Stop right there! I am not interested, and I don't want this to go any further."

Clarity is important. You don't want the other to be in any doubt about what you are saying No to. "Stop doing that!" one spouse says irritably to the other. "Stop doing what?" comes the reply. "Stop doing what you're doing. You know exactly what I mean." "No, I don't know." The way forward is to be precise and operational in your language. Say, "Please stop looking at the newspaper when I am speaking to you." The other needs to understand precisely what you are asking them to stop doing.

Be firm *and* polite. "Please stop teasing me," announced seven-year-old Emma to her classmate Izzy, who was making fun of Emma. The tone was serious. It had an immediate effect. I watched Izzy go over to Emma, apologize, and give her a hug. If seven-year-olds can do this, so can we.

The word *No* can also be used to stop offensive behavior. Interestingly, *No* can attract more help if you are being attacked than even the word *help*. So say the trainers at Impact Bay Area, the organization that trains women in self-defense. Shouting "No!" attracts the attention of others naturally and recruits any help that may be available in earshot. Equally important, the trainers say, "saying No is a way for you to communicate with yourself. It forces you to breathe, which breaks the freeze response. It gathers your energy. It gets your adrenaline going. It reminds you of the [self-defense] class, your muscle memory, the support of the line [your peers], and the fact that you have the right to fight for your own safety. Most attackers are looking for easy victims. They're not looking for a fight, not even a verbal one. Saying No makes you a less attractive target. Submitting and being nice to attackers in the hope that they will be nice to you in return is not the safest strategy."

Saying "No!" helps you gather your energy, reminds you of your right to say No, draws attention, and expresses your power.

"Hold On/Whoa/Wait a Minute!"

The words *No* and *stop* are sometimes too abrupt or harsh. There are other ways to interrupt behavior that are easier on the relationship, such as "Hold on!" "Whoa!" and "Wait a minute!" Sometimes all that is needed is to simply slow the other down and call for a pause so that they can reconsider their behavior. "Hold on just a second," the parent says to the two quarreling siblings. "What's a better way to work this out?"

Sometimes you can use a gesture to say, "Hold on." My friend Herman was out for a walk with his wife in lower Manhattan. As the couple was crossing the street at the corner, a speeding car screeched to a halt, missing them by inches. In fear and rage, Herman slammed his fist on the hood of the car. Furious, the young man driving the car got out, shouting, "Why'd you hit my car?"

Herman shouted back, "You nearly killed my wife and me!"

A crowd gathered. Herman was white, the driver was black, and suddenly the scene took on racial overtones. As people began to take sides, it looked as if the situation might escalate into a full-scale brawl.

Then Herman noticed behind him an onlooker, an older black man. The man's hand, palm down, was slowly moving up and down, as if to say to the young driver, "Whoa ... think about what you are doing." The young man saw the old man's signal, visibly struggled to control himself, then suddenly walked back to his car, got in, and drove off without another word.

In this high-speed world of ours, "Slow down" is one No phrase I personally find useful to say to myself when I am taking on too much or going too fast.

"That Is Not OK/That Is Not Appropriate/ That Is Not Allowed"

Sometimes what is needed is a simple neutral announcement that the other's behavior is not appropriate. "That's not OK" has a matter-of-fact sound to it which simultaneously draws a clear line between what is OK and what is not while distinguishing between the person and their behavior. They are OK, but their behavior is not. Affirming a standard of behavior depersonalizes your No. "I'm sorry, but cell phones are not allowed in this hospital wing," takes the sting out of being admonished.

Celia Carrillo, a teacher in a tough neighborhood school who was previously quoted describing how she lays down the law that no one in her classroom will call anyone else names, explains what happens after the first month of establishing that policy: "Before you know it, they are saying to each other, 'That is not appropriate behavior. That is not allowed in here.' It's really rewarding to hear the kids say that to one another." And it works, Ms. Carrillo adds. "In the classroom, I don't have many discipline problems."

"It's Not OK for Me/This Doesn't Work for Me"

If you are concerned that the other may feel you are lecturing or preaching correct behavior to them, you can choose to turn the "Not OK" phrase into an *I*-statement, as in "It's not OK for me." In dealing with a co-worker who shouts insults at you, look the person in the eye, lower your voice, slow your speech, intensify your tone, and say, "Please stop! I can take criticism, but this kind of talk does not work for me. If you have an issue, let us talk it over in a professional manner." Framing the "not OK" as an *I*-statement can get your point across without hurting the relationship.

"That's Enough"

Enough is an interesting word. You are not judging the other for their past behavior but simply stating that right now you've experienced enough. It is time to stop. "That's enough roughhousing for today," announces the parent to the kids. Having reached your limit, you are setting a limit. In the midst of a civil war in Asia where I was involved as a third party, the democratic movements, fed up with emergency rule by an authoritarian government, adopted the motto "Enough is enough." *Enough* conveys your commitment without attacking.

Saying No Without "No"

The word *No* can sometimes be a blunt instrument, triggering feelings of shame and rejection in the other. It can also be a fighting word, engendering instant resistance and provoking the other to react. *No* lends itself to abuse and overuse, particularly with children, and thus begins to lose its power and credibility. Children come to ignore it or to think it really means "maybe."

Precisely because *No* is such a powerful word, it needs to be used carefully, intentionally, and sparingly. Sometimes it is better to use other words to communicate the same message. On occasion, it is possible to say No effectively without actually saying the word. Consider the following examples:

- In the middle of a medical consultation, a five-year-old girl insists to her father that she wants to leave. "Honey, we are going to stay," quietly responds the father.
- In a bid to bring the price down, a customer insists on unbundling the product that the cleaning company provides, separating the cleaning products from the training and management services. "Our product comes as a package," replies the company rep.
- Faced with a barrage of angry insults across the telephone from a key investor, the hotel executive says calmly, "Peter, we'll

call you back tomorrow," and hangs up the phone—in effect saying No to his behavior.

In each case, the meaning and power of the No come across clearly, but without the use of the word. The No remains implied and unspoken.

One option is to focus on the initial Yes and the final Yes, leaving the No implied. Faced with a long drive with a friend whose talkativeness gets on your nerves, you announce, "After the day I've had today, I'm feeling a need for some peace and quiet. What do you say we just listen quietly to some music on the ride up?" In other words, simply make an *I*-statement and follow up with a proposal.

Another option is to reframe your No as a Yes. Instead of telling your child, "No playing until you finish your homework," say, "You can play as soon as you finish your homework." Instead of telling your co-worker, "I can't help you until I complete this assignment," say, "I'd be happy to help you after I complete this assignment." Instead of telling your friend, "I'm not going with you to the game," say, "I'll catch you after the game." In other words, put your focus on the positive while creating the boundary you need.

There are cultures, principally in East Asia, that go to great lengths to devise ways of saying No without actually using that word to avoid causing shame and to help the other save face. Not using the word, however, does not mean that they do not say No. They just find indirect means, such as using third parties or subtle signs. This may lead to confusion for those not well versed in the semiotics of a different culture.

During some work I once did with a major U.S. automotive company, I heard the story of how one of the top executives paid a visit to South Korea and met with the president of a Korean auto manufacturer. The U.S. company at that point owned a 10 percent share of the Korean company, and the executive proposed to his Korean counterpart that they increase that share to 50 percent. "That is not impossible," replied the Korean executive politely.

Parsing that response, the U.S. executive thought, " 'That is not impossible' means that it *is* possible." Upon his return to Detroit, therefore, he dispatched a top-level team to Seoul to negotiate the deal. For two weeks, the team sat there, every meeting they scheduled inexplicably postponed. Finally, one Korean manager took his U.S. counterpart aside and quietly explained that "It is not impossible" was just a polite way of saying "Over my dead body."

The basic point to remember is that while the word *No* can sometimes remain unspoken, the *intention* still needs to be conveyed clearly and powerfully.

A Shield of Protection

If I had to sum up the art of the Positive No in a metaphor, I would describe it as a shield—a shield of protection. A shield protects you and your Yes without hurting the other. A negative No, by contrast, is a sword—a sword of rejection. It attacks without concern for relationship.

As tempting as it may be to reject and to attack when you say No, remember that your true purpose is to protect and to defend. It is not to harm the other, but rather to save yourself from harm. To protect without rejecting—that is the essence of a Positive No.

A Positive No does not stop with No, however. There is a third basic element: a positive proposal. That is the subject of the next chapter.

Chapter Six

PROPOSE A YES

"Do not be afraid to go out on a limb ... That's where the fruit is."

—*Old Proverb*

Once you have said No, it is tempting to leave it at that and think you have done your job: "Whew! I've said No." But this is not enough. There remains the third essential part of a Positive No: to propose a *Yes?*

Perhaps the most common mistake in saying No is to stop there and overlook the opportunity to propose a positive outcome. In response to the other's demand, we say what we *won't* do but don't say what we *will* do. In response to the other's behavior, we tell them what we *don't* want them to do but forget to tell them what we *do* want them to do.

Remember that saying No is an exercise in persuasion, not just communication. You want the other to accept your No. You want them to change their behavior. And often you want to keep the relationship. This is your chance to make your No persuasive—to make it easier for the other to do what you would like them to do.

The third essential part of a Positive No is a *Yes?* Just as a Positive No begins with a *Yes!,* so it ends with a *Yes?* If the first Yes is an affirmation of your core interests, this second Yes is an invitation to a positive outcome. As you close one door with your No, you open another with your second Yes, as if to say, "Will you come through the door with me?"

As You Close One Door, Open Another

Once I was watching the film *Hook* with my daughter Gabriela, then five years old. In one scene, Captain Hook says vehemently to Peter Pan, "I hate you! I hate you! I hate you!" My daughter looked up and commented: "He shouldn't say that. He should say, 'I don't like you but I'll play with you sometimes.'" The wisdom of opening a door is known to five-year-olds but often forgotten in adulthood.

To close the door and then reopen the same door can confuse your message and weaken your No. But to close one door and open a *second* door, as you keep the first closed, can actually clarify and strengthen your No.

Consider a significant turning point in the civil rights movement. In Nashville, Tennessee, in the winter and spring of 1960, black students were sitting in at lunch counters in downtown department stores, hitherto reserved for whites only. After a bomb exploded at the home of a leading black lawyer, narrowly missing killing him and his family, hundreds of students and citizens spontaneously began a protest walk to the city courthouse. There on the courthouse steps, in front of the massed crowd, the protesters met with the mayor, Ben West. A young black minister angrily admonished Mayor West. West heatedly defended his record.

Then a twenty-two-year-old black woman, Diane Nash, interceded with a question. She asked the mayor if he felt it was "wrong to discriminate against a person solely on the basis of his race or color." West replied that he "could not agree that it was morally right for someone to sell them merchandise and refuse them service." Nash followed up by asking if he thought the lunch counters should be desegregated. West hesitated and dodged the question, but Nash persisted: "Then, Mayor, do you *recommend* that the lunch counters be desegregated?" When West said "Yes," the crowd instantly broke into applause and the protesters could not restrain themselves from hugging the mayor. The mayor's acceptance led directly to the desegregation of the lunch counters, a major victory in the struggle for civil rights.

While everyone else stopped at saying No to the mayor, Diane Nash went a step further and invited him to say Yes. She opened a door, and Mayor West stepped through it.

A No alone can easily cause the other a great deal of frustration, and you may end up suffering the consequences as they react angrily to you. They may feel they are being pushed up against a wall with nowhere to go—as Mayor Ben West probably felt when confronted with the minister's anger. If you open a door, however, as Diane Nash did with her persistent questions, you offer the other a way out and all your power can be deployed in persuading them to take it. In short, rather than working to frustrate the other, focus on *redirecting* their attention to a positive outcome.

Making a positive proposal has another great merit: it shows respect for the other and their needs. They will be much more likely to accept your No and agree to respect your interests if you can figure out a way to address theirs. That is how persuasion works.

And finally, though this may sound odd at first, making a proposal gives the *other* a chance to say No to *you*. Instead of leaving them in the uncomfortable position of the one who is rejected, you can turn the tables and offer them the opportunity to turn down your request. It diminishes the sting of rejection that leads to a destructive backlash. It balances the situation from a psychological perspective, introducing a symmetry that can be helpful in restoring a healthy relationship. Just giving them the opportunity to say No, respecting their right to decide, may paradoxically make it easier for them in the end to say Yes. And if they say No to your proposal, consider it part of the challenge; indeed, the next three chapters will discuss ways to transform their resistance into acceptance.

Do not mistake the making of a proposal for a softening of your No. As Diane Nash's example makes clear, a good proposal makes your No more powerful and effective, not less. It is essential that you do not send mixed signals or offer false hope to the other. Your proposal needs to be entirely consistent with your No: like your No, your proposal should be rooted in your initial *Yes!*

A positive proposal is a practical solution—specific, realistic, and constructive. It can take several forms. If you are saying No to a demand, your proposal may take the form of offering a third option. If you are saying No to an objectionable behavior, your proposal may take the form of making a constructive request for a change in behavior. Or, if No is complete and sufficient, your proposal may take the minimalist form of simply asking the other to accept your No. Let us examine each of these three forms in turn.

Saying No to Demands: Offer a Third Option

If the other is making an inappropriate or unwanted demand, you do not want to say Yes. Yet, because of the importance of your relationship, you do not want to say No cursorily either. In this case, consider saying, "What about another option instead?" In other words, couple your No with a positive solution that addresses *their* needs while still meeting *yours*.

Contrast how two different people I know handled the challenge of saying No to getting a dog. In the first case, a father was saying No to his children and wife, who badly wanted a dog. As he describes it, "I said, 'I don't *like* dogs! Don't like them in the house. In *our* family, we don't *need* a dog.' My kids said, 'We need a new dad.' The result was we ended up getting *two* big dogs. Although I was OK with it in the end, it was probably the most ineffective No I ever said."

In the second case, a wife was saying No to her husband's plan to get a dog. She countered with a clear statement of the conditions her husband would have to accept: "We can get a dog if, one, you make sure it doesn't chew the furniture; two, you agree to put up a fence; and three, you figure out how to manage it while we're on vacation." She put the responsibility on her husband to figure out the solution. In the end, they did get a dog and the arrangement worked.

Invent Options for Mutual Gain

Just as the wife did, you can invent an option for mutual gain harnessing your natural creativity. Don't assume the solution is either-or: either you are satisfied or the other is. Often, you can generate a both-and solution that leaves everyone better off.

Imagine that a key employee walks into your office one day and asks you for a raise. You assume she wants more money and, since the budget is already squeezed, your immediate answer to the request is No. You tell her that there's no money in the budget. She walks out of your office looking unhappy, and when you think about it later, you realize that you are not very happy either. You don't want a demoralized employee who might consider looking for a job elsewhere. So you think about possible options that stay within your budget but that also address your employee's needs.

You know that she is seeking more recognition, responsibility, and challenges that will lead to a significant promotion. She also has financial needs—a son who is about to enter college, with all the high costs of tuition that entails. A number of possible options begin to emerge:

• *Recognition.* What about a new title that would give her more validation and respect from the outside world? What about travel to a conference to represent your organization?

• *More responsibility.* What about participating in a new high-visibility project that is vital to the organization's future?

• *College tuition.* What about checking with human resources to see if a tuition loan might be arranged? Or perhaps you can help her locate scholarship opportunities.

Other options may emerge as well, depending on the particulars of your employee and your company's resources. Creating a third option in this manner helps you break out of the false dualism of Yes or No. It shows you value the other enough to try to address their concerns as best you can. It shifts the emphasis from the negative to the positive, from what can't be done to what *can* be done. It shows your good faith and interest in helping the other meet their needs—but not at the expense of your own.

If you personally are not available to help the other, suggest someone who could. If a colleague is pressuring you to undertake a project, for example, you could follow your No with "Have you considered bringing in a freelancer to help you out? I can give you the names and numbers of some good ones." Making a reference and a connection can often be valuable help indeed.

"Later"

Sometimes your major constraint is timing. In that case, a third option is to agree to the other's request but to change the timing. If, for instance, a client is pressing you to deal with their problem right away, you could say, "Unfortunately, I have other commitments today, but, if you like, I can look it over quickly later this afternoon and give you my thoughts on the phone. I can then prepare a detailed written report by the end of the day tomorrow. Will that address your needs?"

One mother I know offered this example: "I was shopping for groceries with my two-year-old daughter, going down the cookie aisle. My daughter asked, 'Mom, can we buy some cookies today?' I perused my grocery list carefully and looked at her and said, 'Cookies are not on my list.' My daughter paused, then pulled out an imaginary grocery list and said, 'But they are on *my* list!' I pondered, then responded, 'We will shop from your list *next* time.' What made my No effective, I think, was that it was respectful and gave hope."

Just as with "Not now," saying "Later" needs to be done with care, not as a guilty diversion when the appropriate answer is a straight No. Don't make a commitment to do it later or next time unless you really mean it.

"If . . . Then"

If you would genuinely like to say Yes but are constrained by circumstances that may change, you can make a conditional offer. In other words, state the conditions under which you could say Yes.

Take the example of Dave, president of a fledgling consulting company, who felt he needed to say No to a prospective new Fortune 500 client, despite his company's need for new revenue.

During his team's initial investigation of the client, it had become clear that the client's fragmented organizational structure would almost surely block any chance of success for an improvement in operations. So Dave informed the client that nothing his company could do would really help until the client had resolved their organizational issues. In effect, he turned down the job—not with an emphatic No, but with a reasoned, clear proposal: "*If* you resolve the question of your organizational structure, *then* I can help you." Leaving the meeting, Dave wondered how his chairman would respond when he told him he had turned down the work. But he knew there were clear business reasons for his answer, and he had wanted to convey the right lesson to the young consultants he was developing on the team.

A few months later, he got a call from the same client, saying that they had taken the advice to heart and had gone through a complete reorganization. The client asked Dave, "Please come back with your team and proceed with the improvements in operations." Needless to say, Dave did not say No a second time.

Suggest a Problem-Solving Process

Even if you cannot think of a positive option that meets your interests and addresses theirs, you might still be able to propose a problem-solving process that could eventually produce one.

A participant in one of my seminars reported that when he asked a customer for a $10 million guaranteed commitment in purchases, the customer replied with an even tone: "That won't happen, but if we sit down and work through the terms, I am sure we will be able to come up with a commitment that is satisfying to both of us." The participant commented: "The No was straightforward and did not give false expectations, and it was followed by an invitation to negotiate," citing it as one of the most effective Nos he had received.

As I have experienced myself in many political and business conflicts, seemingly intractable issues can often be resolved with an intensive problem-solving process. No one at the beginning can say whether agreement will be reached but, during the process, little breakthroughs often occur and set the stage for larger ones. It requires patience and persistence, but it is in just this way that many Nos in large-scale conflicts from South Africa to Northern Ireland have gradually yielded to Yeses that work for both sides.

Saying No to Behavior: Make a Constructive Request

When you say No to the other's behavior, it helps to be clear about the specific change you would like them to make.

While it may seem obvious to you what you want the other to do, it may not be at all obvious to them. My friend Marshall tells the story of a woman who complained to her husband that he was spending too much time at the office. The next day, he signed up for a golf tournament on the weekend! She was unhappy because her husband had missed the point: she wanted him to spend more time at home with her and their children. She had delivered her No, but without the positive request that would make it clear what she wanted.

Consider the case of a neighborhood group that organized to stop an unwanted development in their vicinity. The group persuaded dozens of residents to make calls and to show up at the zoning commission meetings. The zoning commissioners were frustrated, however, and complained that this group, like others, protested against what they *didn't* want but never helped the commission by advocating for the changes they *did* want. In response, the citizens went back to work, reading textbooks on city planning, attending classes, and learning the zoning code. They then returned to the zoning commission with suggestions for specific language changes in the code, which in turn led to the adoption of more acceptable zoning.

Just as the most important rule in fund-raising is "Don't forget to ask for the money" and the most important rule in sales is "Don't forget to ask for the business," so perhaps the most important rule in saying No to behavior is "Don't forget to ask for the action you want." We all too often forget this last but essential part.

A constructive proposal has four characteristics. It is clear, feasible, positively framed, and respectful.

Make Your Request Clear

Requests for changes in behavior often sound like this:

- "I want you to be more considerate."
- "I want you to take more responsibility around here."
- "Please stop being so sullen."

In other words, the requests are vague, unclear, and difficult to implement.

Instead of asking the other to change their *attitude* or *feeling*, which rarely works, it is more effective to couch your request in terms of specific *behaviors* you would like to see. Instead of just saying, "I'd like you to take more responsibility around here," say, "Would you please wash the dishes that you use?" Instead of saying to someone who is keeping their eyes downcast, "Stop being so sullen," try saying with a friendly tone, "May I ask you please to look at me when I am talking with you? It helps me focus." Define your request not in terms of what you want them to *feel*, to *see*, or to *be* but in concrete terms of what you want them to *do*.

Be as specific as possible. Rather than say, "I would like you to spend more time with the family," which may lend itself to multiple interpretations, say, "I would like you to spend all day Sunday here at home, playing with the kids and helping them with their homework." What gives your No its power is not just its strength but the specificity of the accompanying proposal.

In short, offer a positive behavioral solution to your problem. Behavior has the advantage of being observable. You and the other will then know whether or not your request is actually being met. Moreover, a behavioral proposal focuses on what you'd like the other to do, not on who you'd like the other to be.

Make Your Request Feasible

A second test for your request is whether it is, in fact, feasible. A common request to a friend or family member is, "I would like you to stop being so angry." Not only does this request fail the behavioral test, but it may not be possible for the other to stop feeling angry just now. More constructively, you could ask for a first behavioral step: "Would you please sit down and tell me why you are feeling angry?" This is a more feasible request; if the other receives a respectful hearing, their anger might well diminish.

In an example cited earlier, when environmentalists led by Forest Ethics and the Dogwood Alliance were seeking to stop Staples from selling products made from endangered old-growth forests, they made a feasible request to the CEO of Staples at a public shareholders' meeting. The CEO was not at all convinced that his company should stop buying paper products from these forests, so the environmentalists issued a public invitation to him to take a tour of the endangered regions so he could learn more himself about the issue. That much he was willing to do, so he sent some of his executives to take a look. The tour helped educate them about the problem, built relationships between them and the environmentalists, and ultimately led to a groundbreaking agreement by the company to stop buying products made from endangered forests.

A feasible request typically puts more constructive pressure on the other than an unfeasible one. This was one of the lessons learned by the anti-apartheid movement in South Africa during the 1980s. Their most powerful slogan was not "No more apartheid!" It was "Free Mandela!" This simple, specific, and feasible request helped mobilize people around the world to put pressure on the South African white minority government. Mandela was eventually released.

The more you take into account the other's needs and constraints, the greater the chances the other will comply with your request. So select a course of behavior that meets your interests while having the least negative impact on the other's. The more you can respect their legitimate interests, the more likely they will respect yours.

Frame Your Request Positively

As the anti-apartheid movement learned with their slogan of "Free Mandela," framing your request positively makes a difference.

If I tell you, "Don't think about elephants," what is the first thing you think about? Framing your solution negatively, such as "Don't shout at me," tends to focus the other's attention even more on the unwanted behavior and may unconsciously reinforce it, particularly if *you* are shouting back at them. It is more effective to say, quietly, "Please talk to me in a quiet tone." Focus the other's mind clearly on the positive action you want them to take.

A man I know was very worried about his elderly mother, who was living by herself. "It was very hard to say No to her, but living alone in the old house wasn't safe for her anymore. She fell once and lay on the floor for six hours before someone happened to come by. Despite my entreaties, however, she refused to move. Finally, I made her an offer. 'Try this assisted-living apartment for six weeks. We'll keep the house, we won't touch anything, and if you don't like the new arrangement, you can move back home. How's that?' It was easier for her to move in for a trial than to think she was giving up the house. She ended up loving the new apartment, and that made it possible for her to sell the old house." The son changed the focus from the negative ("Sell the house") to the positive ("Try this new arrangement for six weeks").

In other words, don't just tell the other to *stop* doing something you *don't* want; ask them to *start* doing something you *do* want.

Make Your Request Respectful

Even if you are asking for a specific doable change, the other may say No simply because of your *manner*. You may be framing your proposal in a way that challenges the other's power and causes them to lose face. Your manner can make the difference between acceptance and refusal.

It is all too common to cast your proposal as a *demand* or *order:* "Stop that or else!" A demand seeks to control the other and typically disregards their right to make their own decision. It makes it harder for the other to do what you would like them to do. "Stop talking to me while I'm on the phone!" sounds different from "Will you please wait to talk to me until I am off the phone?" While the essential message is similar, the first is an order, while the second is a request. The real difference lies not so much in the words but in the underlying attitude of respect.

Propose an Outcome of
Mutual Respect

Sometimes no solution other than a plain No is available or appropriate. In this case, your proposal may be minimal. You are simply asking the other, explicitly or implicitly, to accept your No and respect your needs. The outcome you are proposing is: live and let live, respect and be respected.

One partner says to the other after a contentious argument, "I ask you to respect my need for some time alone now. Thank you!" The householder says to a persistent salesperson at the door, "I'm asking you please to respect our privacy and not call here again. Will you do that for me?" One friend says to the other after declining an invitation, "I ask for your understanding."

I once watched ten-year-old Ty jumping around and making noise as his father was talking with a group of friends. After Ty ignored his father's first No ("Ty, no jumping right now"), the father said: "Ty, I'm talking to you. Please help me out here. We're having a meeting and I need you to respect it." This time, Ty complied.

Whatever positive proposal you make, you are proposing an outcome of mutual respect. You are offering respect to them, and you are requesting the same treatment from them. Mutual respect is the goal of a Positive No.

End on a Positive Note

Just as it helps the relationship to begin a Positive No on a positive note, so it helps to *end* a Positive No on a positive note. A positive proposal serves this purpose. So does acknowledging the other with a simple gesture of respect. "Thank you, but we don't take phone solicitations. Have a good day." It costs you nothing to show respect, and the dividends can be great.

After saying No, it can also help to express your confidence in the possibility of agreement and an ongoing relationship. "I am confident that this solution will solve our problem and will enable us to forge a strong partnership." Or, in declining an invitation to serve on a committee, "I appreciate your thinking of me, but my current commitments will prevent me from serving. I look forward to being of help in more informal ways and I hope we'll have other chances to work together." In other words, paint a picture of a positive future.

As he said No to colonial domination, Gandhi was fond of reminding the British imperial authorities, during their negotiations, of the mutually profitable relationship he hoped India would enjoy with Britain after independence. He would do so with a twinkle in his eye, for he knew his interlocutors did not believe that India would ever become independent. In the end, Gandhi was right—not only did India become independent, but the two countries continue to this day to enjoy close and mutually profitable ties.

Don't Just Say No, Say *Yes! No. Yes?*

Now we have come to the end of the second stage—delivering a Positive No. You begin with a Yes to your interests, then let your No emerge naturally and clearly from your Yes, and finally follow up with a positive proposal. You start with an affirmative *Yes!* and then move to a matter-of-fact *No.* You end with an inviting *Yes?*

Just as you learn to construct grammatical sentences, so you can learn to construct your own Nos, assembling the various elements in a careful architecture. Take the example of a sixteen-year-old boy I know who was being pressed by his grandfather for details about his sex life. "Listen, Grandpa," the young man replied, "it really embarrasses me when you ask such a personal question. Would you please not do it? And when I'm ready to talk about it, I'll be sure to let you know, OK?" The grandfather respected his wishes.

Just as with grammar, which requires you to parse sentences into their respective elements, so you can learn the parts of a Positive No:

- "It really embarrasses me when you ask such a personal question" = express your *Yes!*
- "Would you please not do it?" = assert your *No.*
- "And when I'm ready to talk about it, I'll be sure to let you know" = propose a *Yes?*

Sometimes, of course, the three elements may come in a different order, or you may leave one implied, as for example in "Could you please refrain from smoking? I'm allergic." It is important to prepare each of the three elements and have each firmly in mind. Then, as long as you are intentional about it and not engaging in avoidance, you can be flexible with how, when, and whether you express each of these elements to the other.

Once you have delivered your Positive No, you still need to deal with the other's reaction. It can be difficult to receive a No, even a positive one. Your next challenge is to transform the other's reaction from resistance to acceptance. That is the subject of the third and final stage of the Positive No method.

STAGE THREE

FOLLOW THROUGH

9. NEGOTIATE TO YES

8. UNDERSCORE YOUR NO

7. STAY TRUE TO YOUR YES

Chapter Seven

STAY TRUE TO YOUR YES

"First they ignore you.
  Then they laugh at you.
  Then they fight you.
  Then you win."
    —*Mahatma Gandhi*

Now that you have delivered a Positive No, it is easy to conclude that the hard work is over. However, even though you have gotten to No, you may still be quite far from Yes. How will you deal with the other's reaction to your No and help them say Yes to your proposal? Now that you have prepared and delivered your *Yes! No. Yes?,* it is time to follow through on it.

The first step in this follow-through stage is to stay true to your underlying Yes.

The Challenge:
Managing Their Reaction

I once saw a billboard in Frankfurt that announced: "The *only* word I want to hear is Yes." That is probably how many people feel. It is not easy to be on the receiving end of a No. Your No may mean a painful adjustment in expectations, a perceived threat to a vital value or need, even a challenge to their basic identity.

Naturally, the other may resist your No. They may pretend they never heard it; they may wheedle, beg, plead, or sulk; they may lash back, threaten, or blackmail you. Your boss may answer you angrily: "I won't accept No for an answer!" Or your client may react with a threat, "Do you want our business or not? Because your competitors will!" Or your spouse may retort, "You can't be serious! After all I do for you, you won't do this one little thing for me?" It is just these kinds of reactions that you may have dreaded, exactly why you may have felt reluctant to say No in the first place.

For challenging responses to a No, it's hard to beat the one portrayed in this conversation between President Lyndon Baines Johnson and his speechwriter Richard Goodwin, as dramatized in the television documentary *Path to War*. Goodwin enters the Oval Office to submit his resignation to LBJ, in effect saying No to further employment. LBJ, however, refuses to accept Goodwin's No.

LBJ (*seated at his desk signing letters of condolence to families of fallen soldiers in Vietnam*): Yes, Dick?

GOODWIN: Mr. President, as Bill Moyers told you, I have been offered a fellowship at Wesleyan University in Connecticut.

LBJ: Well, good for you. Hah, that ain't easy to get.

GOODWIN: No, no, I am very fortunate.

LBJ: Well, don't wait too long to turn 'em down so they can call the next guy on the list.

GOODWIN: Mr. President, I have already accepted.

LBJ: No problem, you didn't know you were not free to go. Call 'em up, put me on, won't give you any trouble.

GOODWIN: What do you mean, I am not free to go?

LBJ: I mean you can't go! I can't get along without you! That makes you a pretty big fellow. How big a fellow are you gonna be with some fellowship?

GOODWIN (*squirming anxiously in his chair*): Well, you got along without me before I came.

LBJ: You want more money? I got plenty of money. I'll arrange a payment from the Johnson Foundation.

GOODWIN: Money isn't the issue, Mr. President—this is something I want to do.

LBJ: Well, it ain't gonna be! So make the call!

GOODWIN (*standing up*): Mr. President, I, ah, I'm very sorry.

LBJ: Now, Dick, you either stay here with me or you go over to the Pentagon and get yourself a pair of shiny black boots. There's a statute—I asked McNamara—says we can draft specialists vital to the national interest. And that is what I'll do! If you won't serve here, you know where I can send you.

GOODWIN: You'd make me a general?

LBJ: Oh, you don't want to be a general. You'll want to be a private, Marine infantry…that's where the action is. I know you like to be around the action! That's why you stayed around here so long! You listen to me, Dick. You go ahead and take your fellowship but your hands are all over this [*showing him the letters*], you, and Moyers, and Bundy, and everyone else talking about jumping ship! Most of all *you*! You put your name all over the Great Society and you put the tunes to the words of war too! Hiding out on some college campus or anything else you ever do is never going to change that! *Dismissed!*

LBJ uses a powerful combination of cajoling, flattery, and bribery, and when these do not work, he threatens Goodwin's personal survival. Fortunately, most situations will not be as challenging as this one, but many of them will contain similar elements. This is a true test of strength for your No, the time when it is easiest to falter.

How can you contain the other's strong reaction to your No and transform it into acceptance?

Understand the Stages
to Acceptance

The first step is to understand that the other may need time to process your No. In saying No, you are presenting them with a new and unpleasant reality. In effect, you are delivering bad news. Understanding that there are a series of emotional stages people naturally go through when hearing bad news can help you learn how to handle the other's reaction.

In the 1970s, Swiss psychiatrist Elisabeth Kübler-Ross published her research on the rough sequence of emotional reactions people typically experience when confronted with catastrophic news such as the news they are dying. While coming to terms with a No is usually a less dire situation, nonetheless a No does confront us with potential loss and all the attendant emotions. We can learn from Kübler-Ross's work and adapt it very loosely for our purposes. There is no lockstep order, and the pattern will of course vary from person to person. The general stages are avoidance, denial, anxiety, anger, bargaining, sadness, and acceptance.

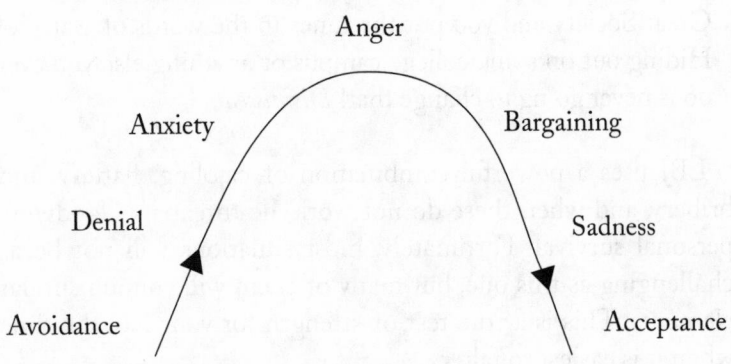

CURVE OF ACCEPTANCE

Think of LBJ for a moment. He starts by avoiding the issue of Dick Goodwin's resignation: "Well, don't wait too long to turn 'em down so they can call the next guy on the list." When Goodwin brings it up again, he goes into active denial: "No problem, you didn't know you were not free to go." As Goodwin persists, LBJ moves into the stages of anxiety and anger: "I mean you can't go! I can't get along without you!" Then LBJ begins to bargain: "You want more money? I got plenty of money." When that doesn't yield the desired effect on Goodwin, LBJ explodes with anger.

Take a business situation. Imagine you have an important client who wants you to accomplish a project in a time frame that you know is unrealistic. You take it upon yourself to explain how it is not possible for you to do the job in the time allotted. This is bad news that your client does not want to hear.

At first your client may deny there is a problem: "I don't know what the problem is. You can do it! I am sure you can!" Suppose you persist in explaining why the deadline is not feasible. This time, your client may get visibly anxious: "It has to be done by then or else I'm in hot water." Anxiety may turn into anger: "If you hadn't taken so long getting back to me with your proposal, we'd have enough time!" Anger generates threats: "If you want to keep our business, you'll find a way to get it done!" You are the bearer of ill tidings, and the game easily turns into "If you don't like the message, kill the messenger!"

Now, you would understandably prefer that the other proceed directly to easy acceptance of the bad news. But human beings are not machines; they have emotional reactions, and those reactions take time to process.

While you may not be able to stop the natural sequence of emotions from unfolding, you can help the other move through these emotions so that they will more easily come to accept your No.

The simplest action you can take is to control your own

natural reactions. Remember that you cannot influence the other's behavior unless you can first influence your own.

Don't Yield, Don't Attack

The moment after we deliver our No is when we may be most vulnerable to wavering. We may be feeling guilty and unsteady, fearful of hurting the other's feelings. It is challenging to stick to No under these circumstances.

I certainly find it so. When I travel away from home, I like to read a bedtime story to my daughter Gabriela over the phone. Like most small children, she is an able negotiator, and she is not at all impressed that she is dealing with a negotiation specialist.

> "One more page and then time to sleep, OK?" I say.
> "Awww...three more," she replies.
> "OK, two more," I say.
> "OK."
> At the end of the two pages, I say, "That's it."
> "Wait a minute, that's not two pages," she says.
> "Yes it is," I say, "We just read page ten and page eleven."
> "I meant two whole pages, front and back."
> "Wait a minute."
> "Awww, just this one time, pretty please, Papi."

And so it goes. Even though I know better, I still find it hard to say No, partly because I feel guilty about being away from home so much.

We may also feel a strong temptation to yield if the other reacts with anger, as LBJ did. We may fear that the level of intensity will keep rising until it results in an explosion that ends the possibility of agreement or ongoing relationship. To relieve this fear, we shift from the mode of assertion into the mode of accommodation at the expense of our needs and values. *But yielding your principles under pressure is not wise.*

One of the most tragic examples of this kind of accommodation under pressure was the teleconference that took place on January 27, 1986, the night before the launch of the space shuttle *Challenger*. When asked by NASA, engineers at the company that manufactured the rocket boosters recommended not proceeding with the launch, presenting data that the O-rings might fail at the expected cold temperatures. But when the NASA official expressed shock and displeasure, the engineers' managers called a hasty caucus and changed the No into a Yes, approving the launch. The end result: the launch went ahead on January 28, the O-rings on the rocket boosters failed, and the rocket exploded, killing the seven astronauts, just as the engineers had feared would happen.

The usual alternative to yielding under pressure is to counterattack. It is easy to lash out and meet fire with fire. "You came to me too late!" the supplier reprimands the customer. Yet counterattacking usually only makes the other angrier and more likely to reject our No. We are now in a shouting match and our positive proposal is history. As Gandhi said, "An eye for an eye and we all go blind."

It is instructive to remember the legend of Hercules. As he was setting out one day to accomplish one of his twelve labors, he was surprised on the road by a strange-looking beast that suddenly reared its head and threatened him. Hercules reacted by striking the beast with his club. To Hercules' surprise, the beast did not run away but instead grew three times bigger and became even more threatening. Hercules struck the beast again, this time redoubling his efforts. But the harder and faster Hercules struck, the more the beast grew, until it was a monster occupying the entire road. Suddenly the goddess Athena appeared by Hercules' side. "Stop, Hercules!" she cried out. "Can't you see? This monster's name is Strife. Hit it and you will make it grow. Leave it be and it will return to its original size."

As Athena reminds Hercules, the key is not to overreact but to stay on track. Leave Strife alone. Whether you attack or yield, you are reacting. You are off track, no longer focused on the prize—the protection of your core interests and needs. Yielding rewards the other's abusive behavior, and counterattacking reinforces it. In either case, you interrupt the other's process of accepting our No.

The choice is yours. The moment you react to the other's reaction, you are initiating an action-reaction cycle that can go on forever. The alternative is not to react but rather to *stay true* to your underlying Yes. Keep your focus on what matters to you. In other words, go to the balcony.

Go to the Balcony

As you may remember from Chapter 1, the balcony is a mental place of perspective, calm, and self-control. Going to the balcony enables you to keep your eyes on the prize.

Pause Before Responding

If the other is in a rage or a panic, you need to be calm enough for both of you. Your calmness can be as infectious as their anger or fear. Remember to breathe—at these moments, we often unconsciously hold our breath and deny our brains the oxygen we need to think well. Take a deep breath or two until you reground yourself. Pause before responding.

The effectiveness of this simple technique of breathing consciously and fully reflects a physiological reality. With anger, our heart rate and blood pressure usually increase, causing the blood to flow more rapidly from our brain to our extremities for purposes of fight or flight. This is not the best time to make decisions. By pausing, if only for a few seconds and taking a few slow, deep breaths, we can begin to slow down our heart rate and relax our tensed muscles. We can then focus more effectively on what response will best advance our interests.

No less a man than Thomas Jefferson invoked this piece of advice during the hot, sweltering summer of 1789 when delegates to the Constitutional Convention in Philadelphia struggled over the principles and wording that would govern their fledgling nation. Tempers frequently flared as delegates stood up for their interests and values and said No. In the midst of this struggle, Thomas Jefferson had a piece of advice for his colleagues: "When angry, count to ten. If very angry, a hundred."

In the modern age of e-mail, the most tempting button on the computer screen is "reply." When the other reacts to our No with an angry e-mail, we may be tempted to compose a retort and instantly hit "reply." Or worse yet, we may hit "reply all," which can rapidly escalate the conflict out of control. The best button on the screen when it comes to responding to the other's reaction to your No is "save as draft." Compose your reply, save it, and then look at it an hour later or, better yet, after a good night's sleep. Then ask yourself what response will best serve your interests. "Save as draft" is the balcony button.

When I am feeling reactive, I like to remember the favorite phrase of a senior surgeon, a participant in one of my seminars, who during surgery makes a point of telling his associates as they are frantically running around: "Slow down, we're in a hurry!" Precisely *because* there is no time to lose, no time to make mistakes, we need to slow way down. Particularly if we want to go fast, we need to go slow.

Name the Game

As you look down from the balcony at what is happening on the stage below you, you can watch the other's moves and admire the cleverness of their tricks and provocations, even as you see through their moves to their underlying intent. If you can think of their provocation as a game, you will be less likely to take it personally. Nor will you fall for their tricks.

Watch how the other tries to push your buttons. Observe your own feelings and sensations. It is not uncommon under pressure to feel your palms sweat, your pulse quicken, your gut churn. As you notice your reaction, you can begin to take control and calm yourself. From a balcony perspective, you can remember that the attack is nothing personal—it is about them, not you.

One very helpful technique to use while on the balcony is to "name the game" to yourself, giving identifying tags to each of the tactics you see being used on you. Imagine that you have just said No to a co-worker, who has been lax in working on his project and is now pressing you for immediate help. You have been working overtime to complete your own commitments and you just don't have the time.

> "Come on," says George. "Please! You're the resident genius on finance. I'll be lost without you. Only you can help me." The game? Flattery.
>
> When you repeat your Positive No, George persists: "But why? It's only a little piece of work. You can do it easily in your spare time." The game? Minimization and slippery slope.

Despite your continued No, the tactics keep coming and you keep naming the game to yourself:

"I have done lots of things for *you*. Now please do this one thing for me." Game? Guilt and emotional manipulation.

"But you said you would help me." Game? Misrepresentation.

"So that's what your word is worth?" Game? Personal attack.

"What happens if others find out your word can't be trusted?" Game? Threat.

"I thought you were my friend. We go back a long time. We play golf together. Our kids are friends." Game? Guilt.

"Next time when you need something from me, I'll remember this!" Game? Threat.

"OK, I'll tell you what, just help me out with the beginning and, if it's too much, you can stop." Game? False promise and slippery slope.

"Just wait until the boss hears about this." Game? Threat.

In other words, meet resistance to your No by patiently and persistently naming each tactic to yourself, thus neutralizing its effect on you. You may not catch every single tactic, but naming even a few can help. Naming increases your detachment and self-control, making you less susceptible to uttering a reactive Yes or a reactive No. This silent naming can have great power.

Pinch Your Palm

One of my favorite techniques for staying on track when I am being provoked is a physical one. I learned it from my Peruvian friend Hernán. It is simply to pinch the palm of my hand. Somehow this has the effect of helping me to remember my objectives and stay calm. I recall one breakfast meeting I had with a group of major media owners in Venezuela, who constituted the backbone of the political opposition to President Chávez. They were very angry and upset with Chávez' behavior. When I proposed that it might be in their strategic interest to open up a dialogue with the president, all fifteen of them began shooting skeptical, angry questions at me for making such a foolish suggestion. "How can you possibly talk with a communist, a friend of Castro?" The questions continued for nearly three hours as I kept pinching my palm to stay calm. It was not easy—on many occasions, I found myself wanting to react. But I resisted the temptation and kept acknowledging their concerns and restating my views in a low-key manner. In the end, much to my surprise, the media owners turned around and asked for my help in opening up a dialogue.

If you know it will be hard for you not to react to the other's provocation, consider asking a friend or colleague to accompany you. An ally can silently—or not so silently—remind you to keep your eyes on the prize. An ally can observe closely and calm you if you begin to lose control. Your friend can serve, in other words, as your balcony.

Use the Power of Not Reacting

One of the greatest powers you have is the power to choose not to react.

In one late-night meeting I had with President Chávez and his cabinet, he was in a rage at his political opposition. For an entire hour, he leaned into my face, venting his anger and frustration, insinuating that I along with other neutrals was being fooled blind. Of course, I felt like defending myself and my colleagues, but I sensed that it only would make him angrier. I also wondered to what extent his behavior was a display of toughness designed to impress his ministers. So I simply took a deep breath, pinched the palm of my hand to keep focused, and waited for him to go through the various stages from anger to sadness to acceptance. Sure enough, after an hour, he calmed down and asked me in a somewhat exasperated and resigned tone of voice, "Ury, what would you advise me to do?" That was the opportunity I had been waiting for. I finally had his attention and suggested what I had come to propose, which was a cooling-off period over Christmas so that all the parties to the conflict could spend a little time on the balcony, and the people could enjoy the holidays. Soon thereafter, the president was chatting amiably with me, inviting me to go on a tour of the country with him. The lesson I drew: choose not to react, witness the drama, and wait for your opportunity to respond.

Remember that reacting puts the control in the hands of the other. Not reacting feeds power to you. Nowhere was this principle better illustrated than in South Africa during the political transition from apartheid to majority rule. In April 1993, white assassins killed Chris Hani, an extremely popular and respected black leader. Tokyo Sexwale, a leader of the African National Congress and close friend of Hani, describes what happened next: "The Chris Hani episode was a near breaking point for everything that we had put together. For our quest, for reconciliation, our determination to be a united people, for everything that we wanted to see—the establishment of democracy, end of war, to silence the guns and let children put roses in the muzzles.

"But there was his skull shattered. It was the most unfortunate experience for me, that morning, to have been woken and told that Chris was shot. I ran there (because his house was just next to mine), half expecting that, 'Look, we have to take Chris to hospital.' But when I saw the wounds it was easy to tell he's gone. What do you say at that moment?... There was a choice. You stand there and you can say in front of the hundreds of television and radio representatives, 'To war!' and you would have summarized the feeling of the majority, the overwhelming majority, especially the black South Africans. I mean if you kill Chris, that is the height, the highest height, of provocation....

"We could have ignited a dynamite on that day. By the time Nelson Mandela arrived from the Transkei, there would have been an armed fight. Yes, we were commanders of the army at the time. Yes, people would have followed us."

But Sexwale, Mandela, and their ANC colleagues kept their feelings under control and chose not to react, keeping their eyes on the prize. Instead they used the moment to extract a critical strategic concession from the government, arguing that without a tangible sign of progress, they could not effectively restrain the clamors for vengeance. In Sexwale's words again:

"We used that moment very, very cleverly... to say to [de Klerk, president of the white minority government], 'You give us a date for elections on the death of Chris.'... Because without the election date, there was nothing that we could report to the people."

Over the initial objections of the apartheid government, Nelson Mandela went on national television and spoke live to the entire nation to calm the feelings of grief and rage and the desire for revenge. As Sexwale put it, "It was very clear that night—the president speaks. And that was the end of de Klerk. The rest was to formalize it with an election." That transformative election took place within a year.

Reacting violently would have yielded short-term release but long-term loss. The choice not to react to a grave and tragic provocation enabled Mandela and his colleagues to seal the end of apartheid power.

When the other is reacting strongly to your No, remember the power of not reacting. Sometimes it is because of what you do *not* do that the prize falls into your hands.

Listen Respectfully

Perhaps the simplest way you can help the other move from resistance to acceptance is to listen respectfully, just as you did in the buildup to saying No. Even in the face of the other's provocations, keep showing respect, remembering that you give respect not because of who they are but rather because of who *you* are. Stay true to yourself and your values. *And* stay connected with the other.

As you listen, watch out for your feelings of guilt. Remember that you are not responsible for the other's reaction. Let them experience their natural reaction to your saying No. Don't try to save them from feelings of disappointment or sadness; those are part of the normal process of acceptance. Sympathizing, as nice as it sounds, may lead you to weaken and yield. You can empathize (which means showing understanding) without sympathizing (which means feeling the pain with them). Empathy is a form of respect.

Paraphrase

People rarely feel understood and respected in a conflict situation. When they do, they are often genuinely surprised and start to relax. So keep listening to them and let them know you are listening. One useful tool for doing that is to paraphrase—to repeat back in your own words what you hear the other saying.

This useful technique can be traced back at least as far as the Middle Ages to the University of Paris, where the rule in theological debates was that you had to repeat back what the other had said until they were satisfied you had understood their meaning, and only then could you make your own point. Slowing down the discussion can actually speed up the process of understanding.

If you paraphrase in a mechanical or insincere way, it will have the opposite of the desired effect and will grate on the other's nerves. But if done in a sincere spirit, it can serve three useful purposes. It lets that person know you are seeking to understand, a gesture of respect. It makes sure you really do understand what is being said. And it allows you to go to the balcony for a few seconds and to think before you reply.

Some common phrases to begin the process of paraphrasing are:

- "Let me make sure I understand what you are saying."
- "If I hear you right, you are saying that..."
- "Help me understand. If I hear you correctly..."

Acknowledge Their Point— Without Conceding Yours

A step beyond paraphrasing is to acknowledge the validity of the other's point without conceding yours.

Whereas conceding means giving up on your point of view, acknowledging allows you to continue to assert your point of view while honoring the other's. "I understand your point. It is a valid point. I happen to see the situation differently." You acknowledge their point but don't agree with it.

Consider the following conversation between a mother and her young daughter:

DAUGHTER: I really want a baby sister.

MOTHER: I can feel how much you want a baby sister. And I wish we could have one, honey, but we can't.

DAUGHTER: Please, Mommy. I really, really, really, really want one. Please?

MOTHER: You're really feeling disappointed, aren't you, dear?

DAUGHTER: Uh-huh. (*She begins to cry*)

MOTHER: I'm sorry you're feeling so sad. I wish Daddy and I could fix it, but we can't.

(*The daughter continues to cry*)

MOTHER: It's hard, isn't it?

DAUGHTER (*nodding*): It's not fair. I'm the smallest one in the family. And I don't want to be.

MOTHER: You don't like being the smallest, do you?

DAUGHTER (*sniffling*): No.

The mother here does not attempt to reason with her daughter or give her advice. She simply listens and acknowledges her feelings, trying to mirror back what she is hearing underneath the words. She allows her daughter to feel disappointment and sadness. She honors the feelings but does not give in. That is respect. (Later on in the process, I am happy to report, a solution did emerge. A tiny dog came into the family—much smaller than the little girl—and the daughter was happy.)

Replace "But" with "Yes . . . And"

The normal prevailing mind-set is either-or. *Either* you are right *or* the other is. *Either* your interests will be met *or* theirs will. *Either* you will have your way *or* they will. There is only room for one point of view; therefore the other must be eliminated. This hidden assumption of either-or creates unnecessarily polarizing conflict that only diverts attention from your objective: persuading the other to respect your needs.

You can choose to adopt a *both-and* mind-set instead. The other has a point *and* so do you. The essence of your Positive No, after all, is not rejection of the other but rather affirmation of your basic needs and values.

Concretely, this shift may take the form of replacing the word *but* with "Yes ... and." If your customer demands a price cut, saying, "Your prices are way too high," it is tempting to counter with "*But* look at our quality, our service, our reliability." The trouble is that the other may not really hear you, for the word *but* is a verbal cue that they are about to be contradicted. People do not like to be contradicted, so they close their ears. You are more likely to get your point across if you begin by acknowledging the other's point first and then make your point—not in contradiction but in addition to their point: "*Yes,* you're right, our prices are on the high side of the spectrum. *And* if you consider our quality, our service, and our reliability, I think you'll find that they are very reasonable for the value being delivered." It is a simple but potent change of words.

Say "Oh? So? No."

In some Al-Anon circles, people practice a useful technique for handling the other's reaction to your No. Whatever the other says, they suggest responding with one of three words:

- *Oh?* In other words, acknowledge the other's point in a neutral, nonreactive fashion.
- *So?* Let the other run through all their tactics and tricks and then respond unmoved.
- *No.* Repeat your No.

Imagine an acquaintance is asking you for money and you have already said No. The dialogue might go as follows:

ACQUAINTANCE: I've run out of money.
YOU: Oh?
ACQUAINTANCE: I'm really broke.
YOU: So?
ACQUAINTANCE: I really need money.
YOU: Oh?
ACQUAINTANCE: You've been a good friend.
YOU: So?
ACQUAINTANCE: Can you lend me some?
YOU: No.

It doesn't always need to be that curt, of course, but the practice is simple and memorable. As another way of acknowledging the other's point without conceding it, this can be a useful exercise for those of us who are accommodators.

Stand True Like a Tree

Just as trees know how to stand tall during storms, bending with the wind without breaking, we need to show firmness and flexibility when it comes to saying No to someone who doesn't want to accept our No.

There is no harder challenge in the process of saying No than dealing with the other's reaction. It is so easy to yield or to attack—to meet reaction with reaction. But it's not necessary.

Even in the difficult situation described at the beginning of this chapter, Dick Goodwin, the young speechwriter who wanted to resign, found a way to stay true to his Yes. Despite President Johnson's histrionics and manipulations, Goodwin did not yield, nor did he attack. He stayed true to his intention, resigned, and took the fellowship. And although LBJ retaliated for a while by freezing Goodwin out of his office, he eventually relented and came to accept Goodwin's No. His response to Goodwin's resignation letter revealed his transition from anger to sadness to genuine acceptance: "Dear Dick," LBJ wrote, "I read [your letter] with deep and mixed emotions—with intense regret for the decision it described, with gratitude for the affection it bears, and with a new appreciation for the man who wrote it." He went on to invite Goodwin back to the White House to write his State of the Union Address.

Understanding the stages of acceptance enables you to anticipate the other's emotional process and to watch the drama almost as if it were a play in several acts. Being a detached observer minimizes the temptation to yield or attack and allows you to wait for the right time to respond. If you do not react, you allow the other's anxiety and anger to subside, which helps pave the way to an acceptance of the reality of your No. By respecting the other's process, as Goodwin did with LBJ, you also improve the chances of having an amicable relationship in the future.

If, however, the other still refuses to accept your No, you will need to underscore your No using your full power. That is the subject of the next chapter.

Chapter Eight

UNDERSCORE YOUR NO

"The stronger the breeze, the stronger the trees."
—*Old Proverb*

The year was 1930, the place India. A seemingly frail old man, without position or conventional power, decided to challenge the greatest empire the world had ever known. Colonial domination had lasted for four centuries, and it had to end. Countless petitions saying No to injustice had gone unheard. It was time to use power—Plan B—but how? The old man ruminated for a long time about the right method. Finally a strategy came to him. The empire's dominion over India was supported by a tax on salt, a tax even the poorest starving people had to pay if they were to survive. No one was allowed to make salt, even for personal consumption. The old man decided he would break this unjust law by marching to the sea and making salt from the seawater.

When the old man announced his project to his political colleagues, many wondered whether he had taken leave of his senses. He was going to challenge the empire by making a handful of salt? The old man then sent a letter to the imperial authorities, explaining his No to the salt law, asking them to rescind it, and announcing what he would do if they did not.

The officials laughed. Who would pay any attention to such a demonstration? The best way to respond, they decided, was not to arrest him but to let him go ahead and make a fool of himself.

The old man left his home and set out with his walking stick and eighty companions to walk to the sea, 240 miles away. As he progressed along his journey, day by day, thousands joined him. By the time he reached the sea and made salt, the eyes of all India were on him—and the world was watching. As the news spread over India, hundreds of thousands began to make and consume the "illegal" salt. The imperial authorities soon decided they had no choice but to jail the old man in order to stop the rebellion. It did not work. Within a few months, the jails of India were teeming with over a hundred thousand protesters. The country came to a virtual standstill. The imperial authorities were no longer laughing.

Within a few months, the authorities relented and released the old man. To universal surprise, the viceroy, the king's representative, sat down on equal terms with an Indian and negotiated an agreement. They agreed that people living on the coast could make their own salt without tax. It was the beginning of the end of the empire.

The old man, of course, was Mahatma Gandhi. No one knew better than he how to deliver a Positive No. Gandhi knew the paradoxical secret of saying No effectively: a powerful No draws on a deep Yes, a life-affirming Yes. Salt is a primal necessity, a symbol of life itself. What Gandhi did was to affirm life by making salt from the waters of the sea, as humans had done for millennia.

In doing so, of course, Gandhi drew attention to the oppressive rule of the empire and to the taxation that burdened the backs of the poorest of the poor in order to support perhaps the richest and most extravagant colonial administration on earth.

His positive action was a loud and clear No, understood by the Indian people and the imperial authorities alike.

Year after year, Gandhi patiently and relentlessly persisted, underscoring his No with positive power until the empire eventually withdrew.

Underscore Your No with Positive Power

If the other refuses to respect your No, you may see only two choices: submission and outright war. Yet there is a third choice, highlighted by Gandhi: to underscore your Positive No. Don't *overreact, underscore.* To underscore means to emphasize patiently and persistently that No in fact means No. It means continuing to stand up for what is important to you without destroying the possibility of a deal or a healthy relationship. It means using positive power which, as you may remember, is the power of a positive intention backed up by Plan B.

Although it is good to remind yourself that you *have* a Plan B, resorting to it may be costly to you and can strain your relationship with the other. Therefore it is wise to use a graduated approach. "The best general is the one who never fights," wrote the ancient Chinese military strategist Sun Tzu. It is preferable if the other comes to their senses before you actually have to exercise your Plan B.

So first, *repeat* your No to the other, as often as necessary. If that does not work, *educate* the other about the consequences of not respecting your No. If this does not work, then *deploy* your Plan B.

Repeat Your No

The other may not want to hear your No. They may be in denial or in shock. They may pretend they did not hear you, or that they forgot what you said. Even if they hear you, they may prefer to act as if you had not said No. Sometimes you need to say No not just once but repeatedly until the other gets the message.

Be Consistent and Persistent

Consider the challenge faced by my old friend Emily Wilson, longtime housekeeper for the family of the celebrated economist John Kenneth Galbraith, when President Lyndon Johnson called one day, looking for the professor:

"Is Galbraith there?"

"He's taking a nap and has left strict orders not to be disturbed."

"Well, I'm the president. Wake him up!"

"I'm sorry, Mr. President, but I work for Mr. Galbraith, not for you." And she hung up.

When Galbraith called back after his nap, Johnson told him: "Who is that woman? I want her working for me."

Emily may have been diminutive in physical stature, but she was outsized in her willingness to stand her ground. She understood how to sustain her Nos. Emily knew it is essential to be consistent and to sustain your No in the face of the other's attempts to get you to give in and accommodate.

Take a business example in which a manager had to keep saying No to his boss's continual pressure to fire one of his employees, Patricia. "I was convinced she was the right person for the company," recalled Robert, "just in the wrong role—so I planned to move her into a position with more customer contact. But still

Ron [the boss] kept pressuring me, with a steady *drip, drip, drip* of pointed remarks.

"One night during our annual budget meeting, a group of us were out at dinner. Ron came up to our table and said to me, 'I hope you're prepared to make the tough decision about Patricia.' I decided to clear the air a bit. 'I am prepared to make the tough decision. Are you prepared for it not to be the decision you want?' In my mind, the tough decision was working with Patricia for her to succeed, not letting her go.

"Ron didn't let up. 'Well, think about it,' he replied. I stuck to my guns. 'I'm thinking about using her elsewhere.' Again, he replied, 'Well, just think about it.'

"I went ahead and moved Patricia into her new role, where she just blossomed and is now doing a stellar job. One evening about a year later, Ron came up to me at a banquet dinner and said, 'That was the right thing to do with Patricia. I'm glad we saved her.'"

Persistence pays. What makes it easier to sustain your No is that you are actually sustaining your Yes. In this case, Robert's Yes was to giving his people a chance to succeed and thus make the business succeed. Remembering your Yes gives you strength and endurance.

A generation ago, hostage situations in the United States were often handled by violent methods. The police would pull out a bullhorn and give the hostage taker five minutes to come out with his hands up. If not, tear gas would be thrown in and the police would charge, guns blazing. All too often, people were killed—the hostages, the hostage taker, and even the police. Just think of the tragedy at Waco, Texas, in 1993, where more than seventy people died, including twelve children under the age of five.

Over time, police departments have learned more effective ways of saying No to hostage takers. While they prepare a Plan B, usually a SWAT team that takes up position in case force is needed, the method used in the overwhelming majority of incidents is quiet, patient, persistent negotiation. Much of this negotiation involves saying No firmly and respectfully over and over again.

Below is a snippet of dialogue from one such hostage negotiation in New York City. As the TV announcer described the situation, "Cops say a man armed with a gun has barricaded himself in a house and is holding a ten-year-old boy, possibly his nephew, as a hostage." George, the hostage taker, was demanding to speak with his estranged wife, Annabelle, but she was "scared senseless" and the police decided to say No:

GEORGE: Because I can't live with this anymore, you know, without talking to Annabelle.

DETECTIVE: You're not going to talk to Annabelle.

GEORGE: So we're going to be here for a long, long time.

DETECTIVE: Yup, we're going to be here forever now.

GEORGE: I'm not going to jail.

DETECTIVE: Nobody goes to jail for a gun in Brooklyn. You know that and I know that. I don't want to talk about this jail thing again. I told you over and over, you're not going to go. Even if you go to court, it's probation. And I don't want to talk about Annabelle again because you know my answer when you talk about Annabelle. 'Cause I want you to be OK. I want José [the hostage, a young boy] to be OK. I don't want nobody to get hurt here.

GEORGE: OK.

Note the persistently repeated firm No by the detective as he also made clear his Yes to safety for the hostage, the hostage taker, and everyone else involved. This particular negotiation went on in much this vein for over eleven hours as the hostage taker went through all the classic stages: denial, anxiety (about going to jail), anger (and repeated threats to kill himself and the boy), bargaining, and sadness. In the end, thanks to the persistent and respectful Positive Nos from the detective and his colleagues, George finally accepted the No and the accompanying positive proposal to let the boy go. He then threw away his gun, as instructed, and turned himself in peacefully. For the New York City hostage unit, it was one more hostage situation handled successfully through the exercise of positive power.

Formulate an Anchor Phrase

It can be uncomfortable to keep repeating your No. It may elicit an even more intense reaction from the other. There is also a conversational convention against repetition. "You already said that!" the other may exclaim in exasperation. Remember that your purpose is not, as it is in normal conversation, to give the other new information, but rather to remind them of an abiding reality—your interests and values, which need to be respected.

The key purpose is to help the other learn that your No means No. Most learning processes, whether learning to read or play tennis, require repetition. It is no different with learning to respect a No, particularly since the learner in this case may not be eager to learn.

Sometimes it is enough to repeat your No once for the other to respect your needs—"I am sorry to bother you again, but there is no smoking allowed here in the restaurant"—and the other complies. Sometimes, however, the other does not give up so easily. Think of times when you encounter a door-to-door or over-the-phone trained salesperson. They often play a game, using every kind of manipulative technique to get you to give up on your No.

One key to sustaining your No is to craft a simple phrase, a sound bite, that works for you and that you can use over and over again when you are under unrelenting pressure from the other and your mind may go blank. Think of it as an *anchor phrase,* a way of anchoring your No (and your underlying Yes) in the midst of stormy seas. Some possible anchor phrases are:

- "This doesn't work for me."
- "No thanks."
- "I am not comfortable doing that."
- "I'm sorry, but I'm not interested."
- "We have already chosen a few charities where we want to focus our giving."

Try to boil down your phrase to its most essential. Leave out saying anything that is not essential—in other words, anything that the other could pounce on in order to escape learning the basic lesson that No is No. An anchor phrase is simply a way for you to stay on track and to avoid getting diverted from your No.

I once helped a friend learn how to protect himself from intrusive questions into his medical problems by anxious relatives and friends. We selected an anchor phrase that worked for him: "I'm sorry, but I don't feel comfortable discussing that right now." Then he rehearsed this phrase over and over again as I role-played with him, plying him with pestering questions. The anchor phrase became second nature for him, part of his instinctive vocabulary. He put it to immediate use, and it helped him protect his privacy during a delicate time. One simple sentence can hold you steady as you sustain your No in the face of the other's countervailing pressure.

Use Intentional Repetition

It may seem a little artificial at first to repeat yourself—in part because we are trained not to repeat ourselves. The repetition of your No need not be mechanical, like a robot or a broken record; this can be needlessly annoying. Instead, your repetition can be *intentional*. You can use the same anchor phrase freshly each time, renewed by focusing on your underlying intention— the deeper Yes that lies within you. You can also humanize the repetition with a smile or acknowledgment.

No matter what tactic the other uses on you, your answer remains the same. You reiterate your limits in the same matter-of-fact tone of voice.

A classic example of intentional repetition can be found in Herman Melville's nineteenth-century novella *Bartleby the Scrivener*. Melville describes a scene in old Manhattan in which a lawyer, a person with superior power and rank, describes his relationship with his newly hired scribe Bartleby. The lawyer himself narrates the story, which gives us insight into the mind of a person who receives a No.

> "It was on the third day, I think, of his being with me ... that, being much hurried to complete a small affair I had in hand, I abruptly called to Bartleby. In my haste and natural expectancy of instant compliance, I sat with my head bent over the original on my desk, and my right hand sideways, and somewhat nervously extended with the copy, so that immediately upon emerging from his retreat, Bartleby might snatch it and proceed to business without the least delay.
>
> "In this very attitude did I sit when I called to him, rapidly stating what it was I wanted him to do—namely, to examine a small paper with me."

The entire scene radiates disrespect toward the employee— the abrupt call, the expectation of instant compliance, the failure to look up even for a second to address Bartleby. Now comes the No and the boss's reaction:

"Imagine my surprise, nay, my consternation, when without moving from his privacy, Bartleby in a singularly mild, firm voice, replied, 'I would prefer not to.' "

Notice the "mild, firm voice"—the neutral matter-of-fact tone. It is a respectful No—not "I won't" but "I would *prefer* not to." Behind the No is a clear Yes, a commitment to Bartleby's own human dignity. The boss, of course, is taken by surprise. He continues:

"I sat awhile in perfect silence, rallying my stunned faculties. Immediately it occurred to me that my ears had deceived me, or Bartleby had entirely misunderstood my meaning. I repeated my request in the clearest tone I could assume. But in quite as clear a one came the previous reply, 'I would prefer not to.' "

The first stage is denial. The boss cannot bring himself to believe that the employee has had the audacity to say No. So he repeats his request, expecting instant compliance. But Bartleby stays true, simply repeating his No. This leads the boss into the next stage of reaction—anxiety and anger.

" 'Prefer not to,' echoed I, rising in high excitement, and crossing the room with a stride. 'What do you mean? Are you moon-struck? I want you to help me compare this sheet here—take it,' and I thrust it towards him."

But Bartleby does not react. He stays on track and simply repeats his No.

" 'I would prefer not to,' said he."

At this point the boss is confounded. He has two choices: he can grow further enraged and fire Bartleby on the spot, or he can accept the No and consider the implicit contract of mutual respect being proposed by Bartleby.

"I looked at him steadfastly. His face was leanly composed; his gray eye dimly calm. Not a wrinkle of agitation rippled him. Had there been the least uneasiness, anger, impatience or impertinence in his manner; in other words, had there been any thing ordinarily human about him, doubtless I should have violently dismissed him from the premises. But as it was, I should have as soon thought of turning my pale plaster-of-Paris bust of Cicero out of doors. I stood gazing at him awhile, as he went on with his own writing, and then reseated myself at my desk. This is very strange, thought I. What had one best do? But my business hurried me. I concluded to forget the matter for the present, reserving it for my future leisure. So calling Nippers from the other room, the paper was speedily examined."

If Bartleby had reacted, the boss clearly indicates, he would have fired him on the spot. But Bartleby is on the balcony, calm and nonreactive, master of his emotions, intent on sustaining his Positive No. Even the comparison to the bust of Cicero suggests how his No is matter-of-fact, an objective reality. Faced with this patient, intentional repetition, the arrogant boss, puzzled and even a little awed, ends up accepting the No. The story highlights the power of staying true to a deeper Yes—a Yes, in this case, to human dignity.

The character of Bartleby turns out to be complex and troubled, but his method of saying No is simple and admirable. The technique of intentional repetition might well be called the Bartleby technique. "I would prefer not to" is an anchor phrase worth remembering.

Educate—Let Reality Be Their Teacher

If your patient repetition of No does not have the desired effect, it is time to take the next step and educate the other about the consequences of not respecting your No. By education, I do not mean to imply that you are the teacher and the other is the student. The real teacher is the situation itself. By refusing to respect you and your needs, the other is bringing about a certain set of natural consequences, which themselves can become the other's teacher. Your job is to simply facilitate the learning process, beginning by asking reality-testing questions, and proceeding to warnings.

Ask Reality-Testing Questions

It is generally better to ask than to tell. People usually learn better and resist less if they learn for themselves. So instead of spelling out to the other the undesirable consequences if they do not respect your needs, it is more effective first to ask them "reality-testing questions."

As the name suggests, reality-testing questions are questions that cause the other to reflect on the underlying realities of the situation, the natural consequences of refusing to respect your No. Here are a few examples:

• "What will happen if we cannot reach agreement here? What are the costs for us both if we need to bring in the boss, (bring this to court, end up with a strike, etc...)?"
• "Have you thought about how this will affect our family (relationship, partnership, etc...) if we cannot agree to respect one another's needs in this situation?"

Let's return for a moment to the tragic story of the space shuttle *Challenger* and the conversation in which the engineers said No to NASA when asked if they thought the mission should proceed the next morning. When the NASA official expressed surprise and anger, the engineers' superior called a caucus and announced to his team that "we have to make a management decision." The senior managers, ignoring the engineers' advice, decided to change the No to a Yes approving the launch. What could the engineers have done?

One possible approach in retrospect would have been to address their superior with a pointed reality-testing question, such as: "Let me understand what you are saying. Are you willing to take personal responsibility for overruling the best judgment of your engineers and recommending a launch where, in our opinion, there is a significant possibility that the O-rings could fail and thus result in the loss of the mission and the lives of seven astronauts?" Such a question might have caused the "management decision" to be viewed in a different light.

Reality-testing questions can be a powerful tool.

Warn, Don't Threaten

If reality-testing questions do not persuade the other, it is time to use a warning. You may need to spell out your Plan B to the other and explain the consequences inherent in not respecting your needs.

I once watched an aunt warn her six-year-old niece about an inappropriate behavior. The little girl was jumping on the bed. Her aunt said in a calm voice, "Tania, please stop jumping on the bed." But Tania continued jumping, oblivious to the request. A moment later, her aunt repeated her request, this time with a little more emphasis, very deliberately and calmly: "Tania, I am asking you *please* to stop jumping on the bed." When the little girl still continued, her aunt gently took hold of her arm in order to get her attention, looked her straight in the eye, and raised a warning finger. Tania got the message and stopped immediately. Her aunt accomplished all this without shouting or even raising her voice. Her manner was patient, firm, respectful—and effective.

The other may at first be oblivious to your No, not hearing it. Or they may hear it but not believe it. Or they may believe it but not take it seriously enough. Giving warnings offers the other a chance to move through the process of avoidance and denial toward acceptance of your No without either of you paying too great a price.

It helps to be very specific and clear. In a sexual harassment situation in a work environment, the victim calmly says to the perpetrator, "I have explained to you before that I find this kind of talk offensive and out of line. If I need to file a formal complaint with the human resources manager, I certainly will."

A warning is not the same as a threat. They may seem at first glance to be the same—both are messages about undesirable consequences—but there is a critical difference between the two.

A threat *dictates* to the other: "If you do not do what I want you to do, I will make you pay." A threat is about imposed consequences. The focus is on power and punishment. Threats often provoke a backlash. You are challenging the other's power, authority, and autonomy. Not surprisingly, the other may react with all the weapons in their arsenal.

A warning does not dictate but rather *educates*. It is an objective prediction of the inherent consequences. "If you choose not to respect my legitimate interests, I will have no choice but to meet them in another way, and that may not be what you really want." The focus is not on punishing the other, but on protecting yourself and your interests. The tone is respectful and thus less likely to provoke a backlash.

Here is how one senior executive delivered a warning to a plant manager of long standing who was strongly resisting a much-needed organizational change. "I called him into my office on Wednesday and said, 'I know this is hard and that you disagree with these changes. But I want to ask you to look into your inner self and tell me if the new program is worth trying. Don't answer now, but I want you to take the rest of the week and go fishing and think about it. If the answer is yes, then I want some specific ways you're going to try. Otherwise, you should prepare your resume. It's nothing to be ashamed of, and I will help you. But think about your prospects if every other industry is trying to get away from long runs and inventory. But the first day, just fish.' He came around and decided to give the flexible approach a real try."

Use Logical Consequences

People learn best when the consequences are directly and logically related to their actions. So it is wise to design—and frame—the consequences for the other so that they flow naturally from the situation itself.

A physician group I know was dealing with a managed-care company, representing 20 percent of their patients, which was refusing to pay their bill. Faced with a significant disparity in power, the physician group might naturally have accommodated reluctantly and agreed to accept much less. This physician group, however, decided that enough was enough and took the courageous step of saying No to a big client. They presented the managed-care company with all the detailed data justifying their bill and informed them that if the bill was not paid, the physician group would have no choice but to cancel the contract.

The consequence is a logical extension of the situation. It is logical and legitimate in a business situation that if a customer does not pay, the services will cease. The physicians' motive was not to punish but simply to meet their legitimate interests. Resorting to Plan B would have meant a significant loss for the physicians, since so many of their patients used this managed-care company. But the physicians felt they needed to educate this managed-care company—and the others with which they dealt—that contracts had to be respected. The calculated risk succeeded. Faced with a legitimate request for payment and a serious warning of inherent consequences, the managed care company agreed to pay the bill.

The key here is to find an inherent consequence for the action. You need to relate the consequence to the problem at hand so that the other readily understands the connection.

Put yourself in the shoes of TV producer Dick Wolf when one day the two lead actors on his show refused to report to work, violating their contract. They demanded better food and a gym. What kind of logical consequence might there be? For Wolf, feeling strong pressure to continue the show yet indignant that the actors were breaking their word, the answer was clear: "We made a very simple statement saying that if they did not show up the next day, the roles would be recast." The logical consequence of breaking the contract and not showing up for work is that the producer finds someone else to do the work. After one of the New York newspapers reported a rumor that two characters on this TV show might die tragically in a fire, the two lead actors returned to work.

Or imagine you are a parent dealing with a recalcitrant teenager who has been neglecting his homework, instead spending lots of time talking on the cell phone with friends. What is a logical consequence? You might dock your teen's allowance, but a more appropriate consequence might be to take away his cell phone until the week's homework is done. The purpose of the consequence you choose is not to punish your child for past behavior but to help him learn to make better choices in the future.

Your Plan B may seem like an imposed consequence since it is you who are the key actor. But remember what your Plan B is—your best alternative should the other refuse to respect your interests. It is not a punishment for the other, but simply the logical path for you to follow in pursuit of your legitimate needs. It is an alternative path to success.

Let your Plan B speak for itself. Through your quiet tone and confidence, let the other know you are serious about carrying out your Plan B with its attendant logical consequences.

Deploy Your Plan B

If the other continues to disrespect your needs even after your warnings, it is Plan B time. It is not time to waver. You have thought this through. Your warning was not a bluff. Delivering a warning and then failing to follow through will only hurt your credibility now and in the future. Carry out Plan B—swiftly and without fail. "No," you tell your child who is pleading to go out to play with his friend, "you may not play with Arthur now, no matter how many times you ask. You made your decision when you both chose to pick on Sally yesterday. Your behavior has a consequence that will not change."

Withdraw Your Cooperation

As Gandhi recognized and demonstrated, perhaps the chief positive power we have in a world of relationships is the ability to withdraw our cooperation if the other refuses to respect our legitimate interests.

A famous Greek myth, presented as a comedy by Aristophanes, is the story of Lysistrata. The women of Athens and Sparta, tiring of the constant warring of their men and the death and suffering it brings, resolve to stop making love until the men stop fighting. No matter how much the men plead and beg, the women will not go to bed with them. In the end, in the face of a sustained No, the men yield to the women's stand for peace and give up their power struggles and violence. The women thus successfully say No to sex in order to say Yes to peace. All are better off as a result.

In a work setting, consider the story of an employee who was being bullied by her boss, a university professor. The professor describes her response, and its impact on him:

"I have to admit that, under the pressure and publicity that came along with becoming recognized in my field, I had become a bully with my staff. After all, I was doing such important work! One day my lead assistant said, 'This isn't fun anymore. I want to do something else,' and left. At first, I couldn't believe she would abandon me in the midst of our deadlines. But she was firm: she understood the importance of the deadlines but could not be part of our team the way it was currently run. Then I thought I could talk her into returning if she would meet me for lunch. She came to meet me and even agreed to think about my request—but still she would not return under the existing conditions, although she believed in our work. Finally, I had to look at myself. Gradually, I began to reconsider my perspective and face dealing with my projects without her help. Then, amazingly, after about a month, she actually did come back, because she wanted to be part of what we were doing—as long as I didn't make her life miserable in the process. What a lesson I learned from this interaction!"

The professor experienced all the stages: avoidance, denial ("I couldn't believe she would abandon me"), anxiety, anger, bargaining ("I thought I could talk her into returning"), and sadness until he finally reached the state of acceptance. The assistant stayed away from the job—withdrew her cooperation—until the boss came to his senses and accepted her No to bullying (which was actually a Yes to respect).

Withdrawing your cooperation can be a powerful way of educating the other and bringing about a healthier relationship. If you do walk out, remember that you can do so leaving the door open. As in the case of the assistant, you can remain open to agreement should the other change their mind.

The More Power, the More Respect

Even when you do resort to your Plan B, it is best to do it with restraint. Power can easily be abused. The exercise of power is often accompanied by a spirit of vengeance, an insensitivity to the suffering of others, and profound disrespect. If in the end you would like to get to Yes with the other, your use of power needs to be tempered with respect. The more power you exercise, the more respect you need to show.

Implement your Plan B with respect and even, perhaps, with regret. Instead of punishing your child with anger, it is wiser to spell out the consequences with sadness. "I'm sorry that you will not have your cell phone this week. When you are able to get your homework done every night, you'll be able to have the phone back."

Do not confuse respect with weakness. If you have to enforce a consequence, with your child, for instance, you may feel a strong temptation to relent before the consequence is complete, but this risks undermining your credibility for the future. It's important to consistently enforce the consequence.

Since the exercise of power can easily strain your relationships, use it sparingly. And keep it positive.

Consider the challenge faced by a group of poor neighborhoods in the city of San Antonio in 1974. Although their streets and sewage systems were in terrible shape and there were federal and state monies available for improving them, the city council, dominated by business interests, resisted authorizing the necessary repairs, wanting to spend the money elsewhere. The people in the neighborhoods might have chosen to use negative power to say No and dramatize their plight. They might have reacted with a riot, as has happened when people's frustrations have spilled over, but the price would have been high in suffering and property damage. Everyone would have suffered, the poor most of all.

Instead, the neighborhoods responded with positive power by creating a coalition called COPS (Communities Organized for Public Service). When the city council continued to ignore their repeated requests, COPS resorted to their Plan B. Hundreds of COPS activists lined up at a big bank downtown, each asking to change hundreds of dollars into pennies. Then they lined up again to change the pennies back into dollars. Meanwhile, dozens of other activists visited a local department store, trying on clothes but not buying anything. These kinds of creative nonviolent actions brought much of the business in the downtown area to a halt. With their financial interests at risk, the leaders of the business community spoke to the city council about the need to take immediate action. They saw to it that there was no more avoidance or denial.

The city council and the business community learned that they could not simply address the needs of the wealthy downtown and neglect the needs of the poor neighborhoods. The city council met with the leaders of COPS and freed up the promised funds for improving the infrastructure of the poor neighborhoods. COPS had achieved their goals by using positive power, strong and respectful, to bring the other side to their senses.

Meet Resistance with Persistence

In summary, your Positive No draws a new line, creating a new reality for the other to respect. At first, they may find it difficult to accept this new reality and may ignore your No or pressure you to yield. While you may feel tempted to give in or counterattack, such reactive behaviors will only divert the other's attention away from the new reality.

The alternative is to meet the other's resistance with persistence. Underscore your No with positive power. See your task as using your power to help the other appreciate and accept the new reality. Let that reality be their teacher, not you. Let the other proceed through the natural cycle of acceptance, interceding only when it is necessary to keep the new reality in focus.

Once the other does accept your No, it is time to negotiate an agreement and move toward a healthier relationship. That is the subject of the next and final step of the Positive No method.

Chapter Nine

NEGOTIATE TO YES

"A tree is known by its fruit."
—*Old Proverb*

Now we come to the last step of the Positive No process. It is time to harvest the fruit of your labors. For the aim is not just to say No. Rather, it is to say No and *still* get to Yes. Negotiating to Yes is the final challenge in the process of saying No.

One of the earliest recorded negotiations can be found in the book of Genesis. It describes the prophet Abraham's audacious negotiation with God. When God confides in Abraham his plan to destroy the cities of Sodom and Gomorrah to punish the sins of their inhabitants, Abraham dares to say No to God's plan—positively. "Will you sweep away the innocent with the guilty?" he asks. Behind his No, Abraham is really saying *Yes!* to the value of human life. Abraham follows up his No with a proposal—a *Yes?*. "If I can find fifty good people, will you still destroy the cities?" he asks. God agrees to Abraham's proposal. Abraham persists: "What about forty-five?" God again agrees. "Forty? Thirty? Twenty?" Ultimately, Abraham negotiates the number to ten. While, sadly, in the end, he is not able to save the cities, the lesson remains. With a Positive No, it *is* possible to stand up for what is right without spoiling an all-important relationship. It is possible to say No to even the most powerful being and *still* get to Yes.

The Goal: A Positive Outcome

The goal is a positive outcome, one that protects your core interests. A positive outcome may take several forms. One is an agreement that satisfies your interests and addresses the other's. The agreement may or may not be explicit; what counts is that the other genuinely accepts your No. The outcome may also take the form of a positive relationship—a healthy, authentic relationship that allows you to be true to yourself and allows the other to be true to themselves. Or sometimes it may take the form of an amicable separation.

In my personal life, I learned a giant life lesson when my first wife and I decided to divorce. It was a heart-wrenching process to say No to our marriage even without children. But the outcome, we both came to realize over time, was positive. Today, many years later, we are each happily married to others, with whom we have children. We have preserved the essence of our original bond—a strong friendship—and now our children have become good friends as well. Thanks to generosity of spirit on everyone's part and some careful work in building relationships among all four spouses, new and old, our families are close and sometimes celebrate holidays together, a source of joy for all of us. Of all the delicate negotiations I have been involved in over the years, none has brought me more personal satisfaction in the end. For me, it has been a vivid illustration of how one can say No and still get to Yes. Saying No can actually bring you closer to the other, and certainly into a more authentic relationship.

I have seen similar processes take place between organizations. I think of one participant in my negotiation seminars at Harvard, whom I will call Katherine Taylor. She was the general counsel for a large technology company that was suing a major customer, a big computer manufacturer, for infringement of intellectual property. Taylor was a litigator and in her previous career had served as a public prosecutor. She believed more in using her Plan B—going to court—than in negotiation. But, as she told me later, she had been impressed during the negotiation seminar by the distinction between positions and interests, and decided to give negotiation a chance. So, two hours before the case was due to go to trial, Taylor called the customer's general counsel, whom I'll call Barbara Smith, and proposed they postpone the court date by a week and try negotiations instead.

The two lawyers spoke on the phone the next day. Taylor told Smith, "I understand your legal position, but I'm not sure I understand your interests." Smith proceeded to tell her that her CEO was concerned not just about the size of the proposed financial settlement but about the impact of the lawsuit on the stock price as well. How would the CEO explain it to the shareholders? Taylor just listened and took notes. Then she said, "Thanks, that helps me understand your concerns better. May I call you back tomorrow and explain our interests to you?" Smith agreed.

The next day, Taylor explained her company's interests, and Smith listened. As the supplier, they not only wanted fair compensation but also wanted to maintain a profitable relationship with their customer. Over the next few days the two lawyers continued to exchange phone calls, and by the week's end, surprisingly to all involved, they were able to reach agreement on what was one of the largest intellectual property settlements ever, estimated at $400 million. The key features included a carefully phrased joint statement from both companies that the customer's CEO could use in explaining the settlement to the shareholders, thus limiting the impact on the stock price. It also included an extension of the supply contract with the supplier from three to ten years. Their relationship was preserved. Instead of having to use the costly and uncertain Plan B of a court trial, Taylor was able to use negotiation to arrive at a solution that satisfied her company's basic interests as well as that of a key customer. She was thus able to say No to the intellectual property infringement and *still* get to a very important Yes.

I have found such positive outcomes to be possible even in situations of violence and bloodshed. Take the New York City hostage situation, described in the previous chapter. It ended with the hostage taker's release of the hostage and his own peaceful surrender. The hostage negotiators persistently said No to his demands and threats to kill the hostage and *still* got to Yes. This kind of outcome is not at all unusual—indeed, it is the norm—in the hostage-taking situations that frequently take place in our cities. On a larger and much more violent scale, consider the example of South Africa, torn by civil war, where Nelson Mandela and his colleagues at the ANC succeeded in saying No to the cruel system of apartheid while still getting to Yes with their white nationalist opponents.

In all of these situations, the outcome was not only an agreement but also a healthier and more authentic relationship. In this chapter, we will explore the process of achieving such positive outcomes.

Build Them a Golden Bridge

Twenty-five hundred years ago, the Chinese strategist Sun Tzu counseled leaders to "build a golden bridge for your opponent to retreat across." Although his advice still holds true, I would reframe it more positively: build a golden bridge for the other to *advance* across—toward a positive solution.

If you step for a moment into the other's shoes, you will see how difficult it may be for them to say Yes to your proposal. A giant canyon may separate what they want from what you want. That canyon might be filled with anxiety and concern about their interests, as well as worry about losing face. If you want them to say Yes, your task is to build them a golden bridge across that canyon.

Three principal obstacles stand in the way of the other saying Yes to your proposal. First, they may have some unmet need or concern. Second, even if they personally might be willing to agree, they might be worried about the opinion of key constituents or stakeholders, whose approval they need or want. Third, even if they do say Yes to your proposal, it may not be a long-lasting Yes because the process of saying No may have strained your relationship so much that, unless you can help repair it, it is irrevocably damaged.

Think of getting to this final stage of Yes as a journey. Along the way, there are three Yeses you need from the other—a Yes to a wise agreement, a Yes to approval, and a Yes to a healthy relationship:

Agreement → Approval → Relationship

Let us explore how to get to each of these three Yeses.

Facilitate a Wise Agreement

Your first challenge is to facilitate an agreement that addresses not just your interests but theirs as well.

Don't Compromise Essentials

Negotiation is not just about getting to Yes but about getting to the *right* Yes. You can get to a satisfying agreement only by saying No to other possible agreements that do *not* satisfy your interests.

In the midst of negotiations, it is sometimes tempting to settle for short-term gains and give in on longer term priorities. Effective negotiation requires a persistent focus on what is most important. Once you are involved in negotiations, you may start to develop a vested interest in agreeing with the other even if it does not make sense for you. The relationship with the other, whether it is your spouse or your boss, may loom as all-important. So take a step back to the balcony. Focus on your underlying Yes—the interests, needs, and values that led you to say No in the first place. Remember that you have a Plan B. Do not sell yourself short and settle for an agreement that meets your needs less well than your Plan B could.

In short, keep your eyes on the prize—a solution that addresses your essential interests. Your job is to respect, not to rescue the other.

Address Unmet Interests

If the other rejects your proposal, you need to find out why. What interests of theirs does your proposal not meet? In other words, ask the other: "Help me understand your concerns. Where does this proposal not meet your needs?"

Consider a real-life business acquisitions negotiation. The prospective buyer was a global multinational consumer products company. The seller, whom I'll call Tom, was the major shareholder in a successful food company that prided itself on its environmentally friendly values. After long negotiations, the parties reached an impasse. The issue was price. Tom was asking a full 10 percent more than the buyer was prepared to pay, and he was not budging. Both sides, in other words, were saying No to the other's proposal.

It seemed as if the deal would fall through. Then the vice president of the consumer products company, whom I'll call

Jack, took aside one of Tom's representatives and said, "I don't understand. We've done all the due diligence and the market worth of the company is pretty clear. We're prepared to pay a top price, but nothing in the numbers justifies what Tom is asking. Am I missing something here or is there some other block? What does Tom need?" Tom's representative hesitated, then explained that Tom was thinking hard about what he would do with his life after selling the company he had founded and built up from scratch. He wanted to work to help the environment and was thinking he would create a foundation. He needed the extra funds, that 10 percent premium, to create the foundation.

Jack, the VP, went back and thought about the problem. As it turned out, his company, which had farms and plantations all over the world, was in the midst of planning to create a global environmental council, whose main job would be to make their products more environmentally friendly and to make donations to environmental projects around the world. The council would have access to large resources, far larger than Tom's foundation might. Jack went over to Tom and invited him to serve as president of this new environmental council. That night, the deal was signed for the market price.

Jack had uncovered Tom's key unmet interest—and found a way to satisfy it without compromising his organization's own key interests. Jack had built Tom a golden bridge, helping him to say Yes.

A wise agreement meets *your* essential needs and addresses *theirs* as well. You turn a situation that may at first have seemed either-or (either you win or they do) into a both-and outcome (in which both sides benefit in the end).

While it would be good if the outcome was a win-win, that is not always possible. Given what you are asking the other to do, they may not see it as a win for them. The key is for them not to see it as a loss but rather as an agreement they can live with on an ongoing basis. It needs to be an outcome that takes into account their most basic needs and certainly meets their interests better than their alternatives could.

"I've always taken the position that a deal is good when it is good for both sides," says billionaire Sumner Redstone, CEO of media giant Viacom. "If the other guy walks away as a loser, this ignores the fact that there is a life after the deal and we may need to work together again."

Help the Other Win Approval

Agreement is good, but it is not the end of the negotiation process. There remains the process of winning approval, formal or informal, from the people to whom the other reports or about whom the other cares. It may be their boss, their peers, the board of directors, their family members, or even the person looking himself or herself in the mirror the next day. The world is littered with agreements that were never accepted by the other's key constituents and thus never carried out. In helping the other say Yes, it is vital not to forget who else on the other side must say Yes if the agreement is to hold.

I learned this lesson the hard way early on in my work as a mediator. My colleague Steve Goldberg and I were asked to serve as third parties in a bitter conflict in a coal mine in Kentucky. The situation was tense. The miners were going out on wildcat strikes in contravention of the union contract. Management responded by firing a third of the workforce. The miners kept on striking. A local judge jailed the workforce for a night. Miners were packing guns to work and there were bomb threats.

When Steve and I arrived on the scene, we could not even persuade the union leaders and local management to sit down together to talk. So we shuttled back and forth between the sides for six weeks, listening and carrying proposals. In the end, the parties decided to sit down together and were able to reach agreement. Both sides were surprised and pleased, as if they had signed a peace settlement.

There was just one little detail to complete: the agreement needed to be ratified by the miners. The vote took place a week later, and the verdict was almost unanimous—*against* the agreement. Even though the agreement was a distinct improvement for the miners on the existing contract, the miners still chose to reject it out of distrust of management's intentions. If management was for the agreement, the miners felt, there *must* be something wrong with it, hidden somewhere in the language. It just seemed safer and more satisfying to vote No.

Steve and I had to begin the process all over again, this time focusing on winning the miners' confidence and support for the agreement. I spent the following three months at the mine, much of that time underground, meeting with most of the miners. I listened a lot, mediated a little, and generally helped both sides implement the terms of the agreement informally, without a ratified agreement. Relations slowly improved, and not a single wildcat strike took place in the following twelve months.

It was a good lesson for me. Gaining the trust of those on the other side who must ratify an agreement is not just an afterthought. It is a central part of the process, worthy of as much attention as the process of reaching agreement.

Use the "Acceptance Speech Test"

The initial agreement between union and management that Steve and I helped facilitate failed a key test: the acceptance speech test.

If you are having trouble persuading the other to accept your proposal, try putting it through this test. Suppose for a moment that the other says Yes to your proposal and now needs to present the prospective agreement to their constituents. Imagine the other giving a little speech, explaining to their constituents why this is a good agreement and why they should support it. Write out an outline of that speech. What is the most persuasive case they could make for accepting your proposal? Jot down the key talking points.

Now visualize the other delivering the speech you have written, and think about the tough questions that might come flying back in their face:

"Why did you give up?"
"What did you give up?"
"Did you really need to make that concession?"
"What about our needs—did you forget about us?"
"Why weren't we consulted?"

And so on.

Imagine how difficult it would be to give that speech and face the chorus of critical questions. No one likes to hear that they gave in or sold out, particularly from those people whose good opinion they value highly.

This is the acceptance speech test. If you cannot envision the other making that acceptance speech in a persuasive manner, then you know you have work to do. If the other cannot see themselves standing up and facing the criticisms they might receive, then it is unlikely they will agree to your proposal. Even if they do, they may not be able to carry out the agreement in the face of their constituents' resistance. In this case, you may need to revise your proposal to make it more persuasive—without, of course, compromising on your essential needs. Anticipate the likely criticisms the other will receive and think about the best answers they could give in return. See your job as preparing the other for the acceptance speech you would like them to deliver.

In putting your proposal to the acceptance speech test, you may find it helpful to use the chart below. Identify the other's constituency. Jot down the main talking points, indicating how your proposal addresses their key concerns. List the biggest criticisms they might receive as well as the best answers they might give.

Their Constituency (i.e., their boss, family, union members, voters, etc.)	
Key Themes of Their Acceptance Speech 1. 2. 3. 4.	
Most Likely Criticisms to Speech 1. 2. 3.	**Best Responses to Criticisms** 1. 2. 3.

See your job as helping the other deliver that acceptance speech. Find a way, without artifice or condescension, to equip them with the best arguments they can use to persuade their constituents to accept the agreement. While you might think that this is the other's job, it is your job too if you want to reach an agreement that will actually be carried out.

As described in an earlier chapter, I once spent a couple of days with the senior political and military command of a guerrilla movement that had been fighting a war in order to win their region's independence from the larger state. I asked these leaders to put their demand for independence through the acceptance speech test.

"Imagine the country's president agrees to your demand and goes on nationwide TV tomorrow and announces that he has granted independence to your region. How would the voters react?"

"He'd be in big trouble, but that's his problem," replied the chief military commander.

"Actually, if you want him to make that speech, it's your problem. What can you do that will make it easier for him to make that speech?" I asked.

Thinking through the president's political constraints led the guerrilla leaders to rethink their immediate demand and focus instead on asking for a preliminary cease-fire, which the government proceeded to accept.

Help Them Save Face

If the other accepts your No, they may be at risk of losing face in front of people they care about. Face is often dismissed as mere ego, but it represents a great deal more. Face is someone's sense of honor, dignity, and self-respect. I have seen many negotiations fail simply because the other's face was not adequately protected. Thus your job, as odd as it may seem, is to help the other look good enough to their constituents so that the other will be able to accept your proposal.

Listen to the advice on saving face from professional hostage negotiator Dominick Misino, who was mentioned earlier: "One very important thing you learn as a negotiator is that, if you want to win, you have to help the other guy to save face. . . . I learned that lesson early in my negotiation career when I was called in to deal with a situation in Spanish Harlem. It was a hot summer night, and there were 300 or 400 people out on the streets at three o'clock in the morning. A young man with a loaded shotgun had blockaded himself inside a crowded tenement building. He told me he wanted to surrender but couldn't because he'd look weak. Now this guy was a parole violator, not a murderer, and so I told him that if he calmed down and let me cuff him, I would make it look as if I had to use force. He put down his gun and behaved like a perfect gentleman until we got to the street, where he started screaming like crazy and raising hell, as we had agreed. While he was doing this, the crowd was chanting 'José! José!' in wild approval, and we threw him into the back of the car, jumped on the gas, and sped off. Two blocks later, José sat up, broke into a huge grin, and said to me, 'Hey man, thank you. I really appreciated that.' He recognized that I had given him a way out that didn't involve killing people and being killed in turn. I've never forgotten that."

Cultivate a Healthy Relationship

The tendency after saying No is to drift further apart when in fact the opposite is often called for. A Positive No enables you to have a *closer* and more authentic relationship with the other— if that is what you want.

Your relationship—be it with your spouse or ex-spouse, your child or elderly parent, or your boss or customer—may mean a lot to you, after all. If the other simply complies with your request but the relationship is thereafter damaged, you will consider it a short-term victory but a long-term loss. Ideally, you would like the relationship to be strengthened, not strained.

Keep in mind that, even if you might prefer not to, you may have many other interactions with the other in the future. Saying No may be but one episode in a long series of Nos. The challenge is to keep the relationship cordial while you continue to have your differences.

Even if you do not intend to have a close relationship with the other, consider that without at least a temporary working relationship it may be difficult to implement the agreement that you have reached. What will ensure that the other respects your needs and *continues* to respect them? How will you handle any differences that arise in the course of the implementation process? A working relationship is key to implementation.

Reach Out to the Other

Just as the Spanish banker mentioned in an earlier chapter invites his client out for a very special lunch at his hacienda in order to tell him that the bank cannot help him on this particular deal, you need to pay *more* attention to the relationship when saying No, not less. You need to reach out to the other.

On a personal level, this is precisely the life lesson I learned in dealing with the ending of my first marriage. As my first wife and I were saying No to our marriage, we took great care to say Yes to our future friendship. Before beginning to tackle the delicate issue of dividing up our property, we agreed on a set of process principles that emphasized our joint commitment to keeping our friendship strong and enduring. These principles helped us overcome our differences and reach agreement on a mutually satisfactory settlement. Throughout the process, we stayed in close personal touch, looking for practical ways to assist and support each other in making the transition, whether it was in setting up a new home or in grieving the loss of a parent. While it was not always easy, the end result was more than worth the care and effort we each invested in cultivating the relationship.

While it is not always easy to reach out to the other when you are still caught up in the heat of a conflict, it can yield great dividends. In his memoir, Nelson Mandela recalls his first television debate with President de Klerk just prior to the first democratic election in South Africa: "As the debate was nearing an end, I felt I had been too harsh with the man who would be my partner in a government of national unity." So in making his summation, Mandela reached out to his opponent and said straight to the cameras, "The exchanges between Mr. de Klerk and me should not obscure one important fact. I think we are a shining example to the entire world of people drawn from different racial groups who have a common loyalty, a common love, to their common country.... In spite of my criticism of Mr. de Klerk," Mandela said, turning to look directly at de Klerk, "sir, you are one of those I rely upon. We are going to face the problems of this country together." Mandela then reached over to take de Klerk's hand and said, "I am proud to hold your hand for us to go forward."

Mandela did not shrink from engaging de Klerk in heated debate. But he also did not forget the larger context of the ongoing relationship he personally would have with de Klerk and that all black South Africans would have with all white South Africans. Mandela was not just making an empty gesture to de Klerk. He was modeling for his millions of supporters the importance of reaching out across the divide to take the hand of a bitter political adversary in order "to go forward." Despite their difficult personal relationship, Mandela invited de Klerk to serve as deputy president, and de Klerk accepted for the sake of keeping the peace at a time of enormous political and social change. It was a courageous act of statesmanship for both men and contributed greatly to making the delicate transition of power successful.

Rebuild Confidence

If your relationship has undergone strain or been damaged during the process of saying No, think about what you could do to repair the relationship. The process of healing helps restore a wounded relationship to wholeness. It is said that a bone, once broken, grows back even stronger. That is the possibility to work toward.

A sincere acknowledgment, apology, or expression of regret can go a long way. Here is an example from my colleague Josh Weiss: "A company I was working with had a difficult relationship with a Native American tribe as a result of past dealings. They decided that it was in both their interests to work together. The company came up with a proposal that they thought was very generous. The tribe promptly rejected it without explanation. Needless to say, the people at the company were puzzled. We probed this during the training session and I asked about their past relationship. A company official explained that the tribe had felt mistreated. I asked if the company had included any language simply acknowledging that the relationship in the past had been one the company regretted. They said No, but would include the language to see what would happen. They reported to me a month later that the agreement had been accepted as a result of the new language. Note that they did not even apologize, but simply recognized that they regretted their past relationship difficulties."

Replenish Your Goodwill Account

If saying No has depleted the savings account of goodwill you have in the other's bank, it is time to replenish it.

In a busy world, it is all too common to take relationships for granted and to treat them as purely instrumental means of satisfying needs. The only time the problematic customer or work associate hears from us is when we have a problem we want them to help solve. The only time we are nice to them is when we need something from them. This is clearly a recipe for trouble.

Immediately in the aftermath of saying No, look for opportunities to nourish the relationship. If you have grounded your teenager for the weekend to allow him to catch up on overdue homework, consider taking him out, after the homework is completed, for a treat with the family to celebrate. Go out of your way to include him, and remind him that the discipline is not a personal rejection. If you have a problematic relationship with your customer or work colleague, invite her out for lunch or an event you know that she likes. And don't talk business for once. Surprise her pleasantly. Don't just do this on a one-time basis. Set up a mechanism for regular communication: meetings, lunches, and get-togethers.

If you have had to persistently say No to a work colleague asking for help, look for an opportunity when you can help him and offer without being asked. Or follow Ben Franklin's advice: "When I want to win over an adversary, I make it a point to ask them a favor—something to put me in their debt, and then look for ways to repay the favor. For example, I had heard that so-and-so had a rare book and I sent a note to his office asking if he might be willing to lend it to me for the fortnight."

End on a Positive Note

Just as it is important to start on a positive note, because first impressions count, so it is important to end on a positive note, as last impressions count too. A positive note might simply be a word or two reaffirming your relationship: "Martha, I know dealing with this issue hasn't been easy for either of us. I just want to thank you for your efforts to respect my needs in this situation. And I look forward to working with you on this issue and many others."

In other words, acknowledge the truth of the difficulties, thank the person, and focus on a positive future. No need for sugary words—a matter-of-fact acknowledgment and a simple thank-you will do. The other is more likely to implement an agreement if they can feel good about it.

Ending on a positive note costs you little and can benefit you greatly. In the words of Shakespeare, "Do as adversaries do in law, strive mightily, but eat and drink as friends."

As a gesture of respect after a long political struggle for civil rights, Mahatma Gandhi sent his indomitable adversary Prime Minister Jan Smuts of South Africa a pair of sandals he had made in prison, where Smuts had sent him. Smuts came to wear them every summer—proudly. On the occasion of Gandhi's seventieth birthday, Smuts returned the sandals to Gandhi with a note saying, "I feel that I am not worthy to stand in the shoes of so great a man." In saying No, Gandhi had not only gotten to Yes with a tough political enemy; he had turned that enemy into a friend and admirer.

Say No ... and *Still* Get to Yes

This last step in the process—negotiating to Yes—brings you to Yes. You began the journey by saying Yes to your core interests, and now you end the journey helping the other say Yes to an outcome that meets those interests. The key lies in building a golden bridge, making it easier for the other to say Yes to agreement and Yes to a healthier relationship.

Conclusion

THE MARRIAGE OF YES AND NO

Advice from a Tree
"Stand Tall and Proud
Sink your roots deeply into the Earth
Reflect the light of a greater source
Think long term
Go out on a limb...
Be flexible
Remember your roots

Enjoy the view!"

—*Ilan Shamir*

We have now completed the process of a Positive No. We have discussed, step by step, how to prepare, deliver, and follow through on our *Yes! No. Yes?* As a final review, let us take one extraordinarily challenging situation and see how all the steps can work together to produce a powerful and productive Positive No.

Citrix Systems, a small Florida-based company that pioneered networking software, found itself in the uncomfortable position of having to say No to a more powerful partner—not just any partner, but the most powerful software company in the world. Microsoft was a partner of Citrix at the time, with a 6 percent ownership stake. One day in February 1997, Microsoft announced its intention to go into direct competition with Citrix, making its own version of the networking software. When the news became public, Citrix's stock price plunged by 62 percent in a single day and its very survival seemed highly uncertain. How could a small company possibly compete with Microsoft? Employees panicked, fearing for their jobs and stock options. Clients worried about who would service their software. Investors sold their shares.

But instead of panicking along with the rest, the chairman and the CEO at Citrix went to the balcony and prepared. They began by *uncovering their Yes*—which was to continue in business making the network software that was their specialty and passion. Their vastly preferred option was to continue partnering with Microsoft. So they decided to seek to reverse Microsoft's decision—in other words, to say No.

As a second step, Citrix sought to *empower their No*. Given the great possibility that they would not be successful in persuading Microsoft to change their minds, they thought through their Plan B—going head to head with Microsoft. To strengthen their Plan B and thus their power, they decided to use the $175 million the company had in cash reserves. The CEO then traveled around the country meeting with key customers to reassure them that the company would be around to service their software. None of their customers chose to leave.

Meanwhile, the chairman sought to engage directly with Microsoft. How could he *respect his way to Yes?* Knowing that Microsoft prized technical expertise, he assembled a team of the best technical minds in the company and flew with them across the country to Microsoft headquarters. There he leased four apartments for a year, and announced to Microsoft that they were there to stay as long as it took to find a way to address the concerns that had led Microsoft to abandon the partnership. This was a strong signal of respect.

Having prepared thoroughly, Citrix was ready to deliver a Positive No. The elements of their Positive No were clear. They *expressed their Yes* to staying in business, *asserted their No* to Microsoft's decision to abandon its partnership with Citrix, and *proposed a Yes* to a mutually satisfying agreement that would allow Citrix and Microsoft to continue to work together on the best networking software in the marketplace.

Having delivered their Positive No, Citrix now had to follow through. "I think they weren't sure what to make of us," said one Citrix negotiator, "because we wouldn't give in and we wouldn't go away." They *stayed true to their Yes,* and listened very carefully to their partner. They then began to *underscore their No* by posing a reality-testing question to Microsoft, asking them if they had really thought about how long it would take them to develop a new competing software—months or perhaps years.

Throughout Citrix continued to try to *negotiate to Yes*. Since Microsoft's key interest was to have control over the evolution of a new and important type of software, the challenge for Citrix became how to give Microsoft the control they needed while allowing Citrix to remain an independent company. Listening keenly to Microsoft's unmet needs, the Citrix team worked on developing an attractive solution for mutual gain. They also tried to make it as easy as possible for Microsoft to reverse their decision without looking foolish. Indeed, by agreeing, Microsoft would be able to improve its reputation as a trustworthy partner.

In the end, against the odds, Citrix succeeded. After ten weeks of intense negotiations, Microsoft decided not to compete but to work with Citrix instead. At a joint press conference, both companies announced their agreement as a win-win. That is exactly the kind of acceptance speech you would like the other to deliver when they explain why they have accepted your proposal.

Citrix and Microsoft continued to work as close partners for the next ten years and beyond. As this example illustrates, even in a case where the other is much more powerful than you, it is possible to say No and *still* get to Yes. The secret lies in the Positive No.

Marrying Yes and No

The Positive No represents a marriage of the two most fundamental words in the language: *Yes* and *No*.

The great problem today is that we have divorced our Yeses from our Nos. *Yes without No is appeasement, whereas No without Yes is war.* Yes without No destroys one's own satisfaction, whereas No without Yes destroys one's relationship with others. We need both Yes and No together. Yes is the key word of community, No the key word of individuality. Yes is the key word of connection, No the key word of protection. Yes is the key word of peace, No the key word of justice.

The great art is to learn to integrate the two—to marry Yes and No. That is the secret to standing up for yourself and what you need without destroying valuable agreements and precious relationships.

That is what a Positive No seeks to achieve.

Practicing the Positive No

As I was writing these words in the room of a mountain inn, my eyes fell on a simple No Smoking sign that was phrased as follows:

IN ORDER TO ACCOMMODATE THE PLEASURE OF ALL
OUR GUESTS, THIS IS A **NON-SMOKING** ROOM.

WE ASK THAT YOU SMOKE IN OUR SMOKING ROOM,
THE GREAT OUTDOORS! THANK YOU!

This No has all three basic parts of a Positive No. It affirms the innkeepers' underlying *Yes!* ("to accommodate the pleasure of all our guests"). It spells out the *No* in a matter-of-fact statement of reality ("This is a non-smoking room"). And it leads immediately to a concrete and constructive *Yes?* ("We ask that you smoke in our smoking room, the great outdoors"). It ends with a simple gesture of respect ("Thank you").

Just as the innkeepers knew instinctively, each of us probably already knows the basic elements of a Positive No. It is common sense—or perhaps *un*common sense, since so many of our Nos fail to follow this simple pattern. It is my strong hope that the simple *Yes! No. Yes?* framework outlined in this book will help make it easier for you to say No in a positive and effective manner.

As with most challenges, preparation and practice help. Indeed, once you have practiced the method, it takes less and less time to prepare, sometimes only a few seconds. Generally, however, the more preparation, the better.

Begin by paying closer attention to how you say No. Is your tendency to accommodate, to attack, or to avoid—or a combination of all three? Notice when you say No well and when you don't. With whom do you have the greatest difficulties—your boss, your children, your elderly parents? Observe your unhealthy Yeses and your unhealthy Nos. Reflect on what works and what doesn't. Then try again.

Keep practicing. It is a good exercise to say No at least once a day in a situation that counts. For those of us who are accommodators, it is important to run the risk of sounding disagreeable and making someone upset. Remember that you have the right to say No—indeed, the duty to yourself to say No—when it really matters.

If you are having difficulty, find yourself a coach and rehearse. If you have an important speech or presentation to give, you would rehearse it as a matter of course. Saying No to a boss, key customer, spouse, or child may be among the most important speeches you ever give. So try out your No on a friend or colleague, get some feedback, improve on it, and try it out again. Anticipate the various ways the other may react to your No, and have a plan for how to respond to each. Your friend can play the other person and you can practice not reacting to provocation and pressure. Once you have heard and experienced the great variety of human manipulations, it is easier to withstand them in real life.

Use your friends as supporters throughout the process. Tell them you are going to deliver an important No and stick to it. Commit yourself. Your friends can help you overcome your emotional resistance to saying No and can support you if the other pressures you to back down.

Changing old patterns takes practice. Fortunately, each of us is offered many opportunities a day to practice saying No. Think of it like exercise. You are building your Positive No muscle. With daily exercise, that muscle will get stronger and stronger. With practice and reflection, anyone can improve greatly at the art of saying No.

Giving the Gift of No

The way we say No may sometimes seem like a small thing, but over time it can make a huge difference in our lives, in the lives of others around us, and in the world at large.

In saying No positively, we are giving ourselves a gift. We are creating time and space for what we want. We are protecting what we value. We are changing the situation for the better—and all the while keeping our friends, colleagues, and customers. In short, we are being true to ourselves. Through the simple daily practice of saying No positively, we are contributing to the quality of our lives, our success at work, and our happiness at home. It is a gift we owe ourselves.

Your No can be a gift to the other as well. "Tell me Yes, tell me No, but tell me *now*" is a refrain I have often heard from those on the receiving end. The other often much prefers a clear answer, even if it is No, than continued indecision and waffling. A No allows them to go ahead and make their own decisions.

Indeed, a Positive No can bring us closer to the other, into a more authentic relationship. If we do not speak our truth—our No—we may in fact distance ourselves from the other, as there will always be something important that lies unspoken between us. One friend of mine who was separating temporarily from his wife put it this way: "We needed to disentangle ourselves in order to reconnect." And they found that they did reconnect, in a much healthier relationship. An honest and respectful No can benefit both parties.

Saying No is a gift not only to ourselves and the other but also to the larger whole. Imagine for a moment a world in which Positive Nos were the norm, not the exception.

At home, parents who knew how to deliver respectful Nos to their children would see a lot less destructive strife, and their children would be less spoiled and much happier, as children are when they grow up with firm, respectful limits. Those who are in troubled relationships would find that their marriages and friendships have a much greater chance of succeeding.

In the workplace, managers and leaders who knew how to say No would do a much better job of keeping their organizations strategically focused. People in departments such as finance and human resources who regularly have to say No to internal clients would be able to contribute more effectively to the organization's success. People in sales would know when and how to say No to customers—and would feel supported in doing so. And everyone would be more empowered to create a healthier balance between work and personal life.

In the world at large, if people knew how to say No positively, they would stand up for what is right in productive ways that lead to constructive solutions. The result might be more contention in the beginning, but much less war and much more justice in the end.

Finally, Mother Earth herself would be a prime beneficiary as her children learned how to say No to runaway excesses that threaten the natural environment on which we and all future generations depend.

Life, in short, would be a lot happier, healthier, and saner.

There is no doubt that delivering a Positive No requires courage, vision, empathy, fortitude, patience, and persistence. But it is within the reach of everyone every day, and the rewards are potentially enormous.

By rehabilitating No and marrying it with Yes, we can make a better life for ourselves and for those around us. In the process, we can build a better world for our children and grandchildren, based on integrity, dignity, and mutual respect.

You don't have to choose between saying No and getting to Yes. You can do *both*.

You can say No ... positively!

In closing, I wish you the kind of success that can come only from being true to yourself and respectful to others!

Endnotes

Introduction:

p. 14, All three approaches were at work: Stephen Labaton and Heather Timmons, "Shell's Report on Its Troubles Cites Discord at Top," *The New York Times,* April 20, 2004.

p. 15, This was what John did: David Schnarch, *The Passionate Marriage* (New York: Henry Holt, 1997), p. 124. The original pseudonym used by Schnarch is Bill.

p. 18, According to the sages of ancient India: This passage refers to the Hindu deities, Brahma, the world-creator, Vishnu, the world-maintainer, and Shiva, the world-destroyer.

p. 20, Consider how one group of mothers said No: Ken Butigan, "Walking on the Water," Pace e Bene Nonviolence Service. The article can be found at http://paceebene.org/pace/nvns/essays-on-nonviolence/walking-on-the-water.

Chapter One:

p. 27, In creating: James Russell Lowell, "A Fable for Critics," *Selections from American Poetry: With Special Reference to Poe, Longfellow, Lowell and Whittier* (New York: The Macmillan Company, 1917), p. 276.

p. 28, Consider an old Japanese story: This story is sometimes referred to as the legend of Hakugin Shrine in Itoman City. It is included on the official Itoman website, which can be found at www.city.itoman.okinawa.jp/tourist_info/HTML/itoman08_e.html.

p. 40, Recall the story of Sherron Watkins: Jennifer Frey, "The Woman Who Saw Red; Enron Whistle-Blower Sherron Watkins Warned of the Trouble to Come," *The Washington Post,* January 25, 2002.

p. 41, This exercise applies not only to individuals: A more detailed version of the James Burke story can be found in the article by N. R. Kleinfield, "Tylenol's Rapid Comeback," *The New York Times,* September 17, 1983. To read more about Tylenol's credo, see the article by Steven Prokesch, "Tylenol: Despite Sharp Disputes, Managers Coped," *The New York Times,* February 23, 1986.

p. 42, "the better angels of our nature": Taken from Abraham Lincoln's First Inaugural Address given on Monday, March 4, 1861.

p. 43, "True strength": Taken from an essay by Mahatma Gandhi called "The Doctrine of the Sword." The essay was printed in *Young India* on August 11, 1920.

p. 46, No one understood and demonstrated: Richard Attenborough, *The Words of Gandhi* (New York: Newmarket Press, 2001).

p. 47, "Gandhi taught me at age twelve": The transcript of this interview can be found on the PRX Radio website. "Regarding Gandhi (Peace Talks Radio Series)" http://www.prx.org/pieces/10606.

Chapter Two:

p. 53, To be prepared: Miguel de Cervantes Saavedra, *Don Quixote de La Mancha* (New York: Random House, 1998), p. 1181.

p. 54, "I did not sit at the very front of the bus": Rosa Parks' answers to questions from elementary school students, *Scholastic.com,* January and February 1997. The interview transcript can be found at http://content.scholastic.com/browse/article.jsp?id=5223.

p. 55, A friend once described Parks: Taken from a biography of Rosa Parks. See full article by the Toonari Corporation at Africanaonline. The article can be found at http://www.africanaonline.com/rosa_parks.htm.

p. 56, Consider a real-life marital dispute: See previous citation for *The Passionate Marriage.*

p. 59, The story of "the man who said No to Wal-Mart": Charles Fishman, "The Man Who Said No to Wal-Mart," *Fast Company,* January 2006.

p. 67, There are two kinds of power in this world: Saul Alinsky, *Rules for Radicals* (New York: Vintage Books, 1989), p. 127.

p. 67, One telling example: This story was told in an *Associated Press* article called "Pilot's Advice: Fight Back," written on September 21, 2001.

p. 69, Unbeknownst to the U.S. leadership: Martin Tolchin, "U.S. Underestimated Soviet Force in Cuba During '62 Missile Crisis," *The New York Times,* January 15, 1992.

Chapter Three:

p. 77, There is a real-life story: This story was included in a collection by Ram Dass and Paul Gorman called *How Can I Help?* (New York: Alfred A. Knopf, 1996) p. 167.

p. 81, During the Second World War: From the abridged version of Winston Churchill's memoirs titled *Memoirs of the Second World War* (Boston: Houghton Mifflin, 1959), pp. 507–8.

p. 83, When I'm dealing with an armed criminal: Diane L. Coutu, "Negotiating Without a Net: A Conversation with the NYPD's Dominick J. Misino," *The Harvard Business Journal,* October 2002, R0210C.

p. 83, I have a real strict policy with my kids: Anni Layne, "Conflict Resolution: Stop, Look & Listen," *Fast Company,* August 1999.

p. 84, If they listen to us: Katrin Bennhold, "In Paris Suburbs, Anger Won't Cool," *International Herald Tribune,* November 4, 2005.

p. 84, Respect is the cheapest concession: For more information about Toyota's corporate culture see their company website at http://www.toyota.co.jp/en/vision/philosophy/.

p. 86, Talk to me: From the documentary, "Talk to Me: The Hostage Negotiators of the NYPD" (Investigative Reports).

p. 87, When Nelson Mandela: Nelson Mandela, *Long Walk to Freedom* (New York: Little, Brown and Company, 1994).

p. 89, Acknowledgment means treating the other not as a nobody: For an eloquent exposition on the importance of dignity in all domains of life, see Robert Fuller, *All Rise: Somebodies, Nobodies, and the Politics of Dignity* (Berrett-Koehler, 2006).

p. 89, Consider the approach taken by Bob Iger: This complete story comes from two articles. See "Restoring Disney's Magic: Michael Eisner's successor,

Bob Iger, is off to a good start," *The Economist,* July 14, 2005. Also check out Brent Schlender's article "Pixar's Magic Man," published in *Fortune* on May 17, 2006, for the most recent development in the story.

p. 91, Starting from the other's perspective: Story courtesy of Betty Peck. You can see her website at: www.kindergarten-forum.com.

p. 92, Affirming the other's value: Taken from a radio program called "The Paper Principle: Doing Well by Doing Good," from the "World of Possibilities Program," part of *The Mainstream Media Project.*

p. 92, Listen to the story of Troy Chapman: Troy Chapman, "Through My Enemy's Eyes," *Yes!,* Winter 2002.

p. 93, One of the most dramatic and surprising acts: "Anwar Sadat: Architect of a New Mideast," *Time Magazine,* January 2, 1978.

Chapter Four:

p. 101, Be like a tree in pursuit of your cause: See Richard St. Barbe Baker's memorial website at: http://www.manofthetrees.org/HTMLS/contactinfo.html.

p. 103, When Nelson Mandela: *Long Walk to Freedom,* p. 368.

p. 111, The poet William Blake: William Blake, *Songs of Innocence and Experience* (New Jersey: Princeton University Press, 1991), p. 97.

p. 111, Psychologists have found: Carol Tavris, *Anger: The Misunderstood Emotion* (Touchstone, 1989), p. 243.

p. 112, "One of the most powerful pieces": From an interview with Impact Bay Area trainers done by Candace Carpenter in 2004.

p. 113, She told him the straight facts: Frances Moore Lappe, *You Have the Power: Choosing Courage in a Culture of Fear* (New York: Penguin, 2005), pp. 103–104.

p. 115, Consider a business example: Jim Collins, *Good to Great, Why Some Companies Make the Leap and Others Don't* (New York: Harper Collins Publishers, Inc., 2001), p. 31.

p. 118, When you express your Yes: Personal Communication from Bob Woolf to the author, with direct quotes from Bob Woolf, *Friendly Persuasion* (New York: Putnam, 1990), pp. 37–43.

Chapter Five:

p. 132, "There are moments when people have to say no": This interview comes from an article on p. 4A in *Jornal da Tarde,* published in Sao Paulo, Brazil, on June 29, 2003.

p. 133, Directness has its place: British Pathe Gazette newsreel footage, 9/14/1931—"Gandhi is Here!" Timecode for the specific segment is: 1:01:55:00-1:05:25:00 Film ID: 867.03, Canister ID: 31/74. Available through www.britishpathe.com.

p. 139, The word *No*: For more information about Impact Bay Area, see their website at www.impactbayarea.org/.

p. 141, Celia Carrillo, a teacher in a rough neighborhood: See citation for "Conflict Resolution: Stop, Look & Listen," above.

Chapter Six:

p. 148, Consider a significant turning point: The story of Diane Nash can be found in the book by Peter Ackerman and Jack Duvall, *A Force More Powerful* (New York: St. Martin's Press, 2000), p. 327.

p. 158, A feasible request: *Long Walk to Freedom,* p. 324.

p. 161, Gandhi was fond of reminding: One of my favorite books on Gandhi is William Shirer's *Gandhi, A Memoir* (New York: Simon & Schuster, 1979).

Chapter Seven:

p. 170, In the 1970s: Elisabeth Kübler-Ross, *The Economist,* September 2, 2004.

p. 173, One of the most tragic examples: Philip Bofey, "Shuttle officials deny pressuring rocket engineers," *The New York Times,* February 27, 1986.

p. 179, Remember that reacting: John Carlin, "Interview: Tokyo Sexwale," The Long Walk of Nelson Mandela, PBS, May 1999.

Chapter Eight:

p. 189, The year was 1930: See previous citation for *Gandhi, A Memoir.*

p. 193, A generation ago: Jim Lehrer, "Revisiting Waco," PBS, August 26, 1999.

p. 197, Melville describes a scene: Herman Melville, *Bartleby and Benito Cereno* (New York: Dover Publications, Inc., 1990), pp. 10–12.

p. 204, Put yourself in the shoes: March Gunther, "Crime Pays," *Fortune,* March 21, 2005.

p. 205, A famous Greek myth: Aristophanes, *Lysistrata* (New York: New American Library, 1964).

p. 207, Consider the challenge faced: Cheryl Dahle, "Social Justice—Ernesto Cortes Jr.," *Fast Company,* November 1999.

Chapter Nine:

p. 220, "I've always taken the position": From an interview by Scott S. Smith, "Let Him Entertain You," *American Way,* March 15, 2005, p. 64.

p. 225, Listen to the advice: See previous citation for "Negotiating without a net," p. 7.

p. 227, While it is not always easy: see previous citation for *Long Walk to Freedom.* This passage occurred on p. 617.

p. 229, Or follow Ben Franklin's advice: Benjamin Franklin, *Benjamin Franklin, His Autobiography* (New York, Collier and Son, 1909), p. 212.

p. 230, Ending on a positive note: William Shakespeare, *The Taming of the Shrew,* Act I, Scene 2 (New York: Washington Square Press, 1992), p. 69.

Conclusion:

p. 233, Stand Tall and Proud: Ilan Shamir, "Advice from a Tree," © 1993–2004 YTN. Reprinted by permission. Contact www.YourTrueNature.com or call toll free 1-800-992-4769 for information about products and workshops.

p. 233, Citrix Systems, a small Florida-based company: Kevin Maney, "Tiny Tech Firm Does the Unthinkable," *USA Today,* June 11, 1997.

Index

About the Author

A negotiator, public speaker, and bestselling author, William Ury directs the Global Negotiation Project at Harvard University. He is co-author of *Getting to YES* and author of *Getting Past No* and *The Third Side*. Over the past three decades, Ury has mediated in conflicts ranging from coal strikes to boardroom battles to civil wars around the world. He has taught negotiation to tens of thousands of leaders in business, government, and the nonprofit sector.

Ury is co-founder of the e-Parliament (www.e-parl.net), a problem-solving forum for effective legislation, connecting members of congress and parliament around the world. He also leads the Abraham Path Initiative (www.abrahampath.org), which seeks to create a permanent path of tourism and pilgrimage in the Middle East, retracing the footsteps of Abraham, the unifying figure of Judaism, Christianity, and Islam.

Trained as an anthropologist, Ury holds a B.A. from Yale and a Ph.D. from Harvard.

For further information, please visit www.williamury.com or send an e-mail to info@williamury.com